Very Long Range
P-51 Mustang Units
of the Pacific War

Aviation Elite Units • 21

OSPREY
PUBLISHING

Very Long Range P-51 Mustang Units of the Pacific War

Carl Molesworth
Series editor Tony Holmes

Front Cover
On 7 April 1945, one month to the day after the first P-51s had arrived on Iwo Jima, the 15th and 21st FGs of VII Fighter Command flew the first Very Long Range mission to Japan. A total of 108 Mustangs were assigned to escort 103 B-29s of the 73rd BW in an attack on the Nakajima aircraft engine plants in western Tokyo. Japanese fighters began intercepting the formation over Sagami Bay, 40 miles short of the target, at 1030 hrs. The defenders attempted to avoid the Mustangs and engage the B-29s, but their attacks were uncoordinated and they managed to shoot down just one bomber, with two more lost to flak.

Maj James B Tapp, flying P-51D-20 *Margaret IV*, was leading a flight of the 78th FS/15th FG, with 1Lt Philip J Maher in *Muriel IV* as his wingman. Tapp quickly dispatched a Ki-45 Toryu and a Ki-61 Hein, then noticed a B-29 take a flak hit in its No 2 engine. Tapp recalled;

'An unpainted "Oscar" was in the vicinity. I don't know if he was going after the burning B-29 or not, but he was a fighter, and represented a threat to the bombers, including the cripple. I started a 90-degree pass on the enemy, firing continuously until dead astern. Pieces were coming off and striking my aeroplane as we closed. The "Oscar" didn't ignite, but spiralled into the ground.

'As we pulled back into escort position, the wing of the B-29 burned off and he went down. We spotted six more fighters coming at the formation. All six had dark paint jobs – four "Zekes" or "Hamps", and two others. Maher and I went head-on with those two, and when we passed them I started a high-speed, low gravity turn to re-engage. They started a high-G turn apparently, and the one I got hits on in the head-on pass suffered left-wing failure in the area where incendiary hits were observed. About this time Maher called that he had run out of gas in his fuselage tank. This was our pre-arranged condition for leaving, so we started for the rally point.'

Maj Tapp was credited with four victories on 7 April, and scored again five days later to become the first USAAF pilot to claim five kills over Japan. His final tally was eight confirmed and two damaged (*Cover artwork by Mark Postlethwaite*)

First published in Great Britain in 2006 by Osprey Publishing
Midland House, West Way, Botley, Oxford, OX2 0PH
443 Park Avenue South, New York, NY, 10016, USA
E-mail: info@ospreypublishing.com

© 2006 Osprey Publishing Limited

ISBN 13: 978 1 84603 042 0

Edited by Tony Holmes
Page design by Tony Truscott
Cover Artwork by Mark Postlethwaite
Aircraft Profiles and Line Artwork by Mark Styling
Index by Alan Thatcher
Originated by PPS Grasmere, Leeds, UK
Printed and bound in China through Bookbuilders

07 08 09 10 11   11 10 9 8 7 6 5 4 3 2

EDITOR'S NOTE
To make this best-selling series as authoritative as possible, the Editor would be interested in hearing from any individual who may have relevant photographs, documentation or first-hand experiences relating to the world's elite units, and their aircraft, of the various theatres of war. Any material used will be credited to its original source. Please write to Tony Holmes via e-mail at: tony.holmes@osprey-jets.freeserve.co.uk

ACKNOWLEDGEMENTS
It would not have been possible to write this book without the help of a lot of people. First, of course, thank you to the many veterans of service in the 15th, 21st and 506th FGs on Iwo Jima, and their families, who provided the Author with photographs, documents and personal stories that brought the book to life. Fellow aviation history enthusiasts who made invaluable contributions were Tom Ivie, Tim Bivens, Alan Griffith, John Benbow and Mark Stevens. Special mention goes to author Jack Lambert for his pioneering work on VII Fighter Command in his books *The Pineapple Air Force* and *The Long Campaign*. Finally, the Air Force Historical Research Agency at Maxwell AFB supplied historical records that provided a solid factual foundation for this account.

CONTENTS

INTRODUCTION

The pilots called themselves the 'Tokyo Club.' It was a simple task to become a member. All you had to do was strap yourself into a heavily loaded P-51 Mustang fighter; take off from Iwo Jima (a postage-stamp sized volcanic island in the middle of the Pacific Ocean); fly 650 miles north over the sea – sometimes through monsoon storms – in your single-engined aircraft to Japan; attack a heavily defended target in the vicinity of the enemy's capital city; then turn around and fly home, while fretting over your dwindling fuel supply and perhaps battle damage as well. If your fuel held out and you did not lose your way on the return trip, you landed back at Iwo after an eight-hour flight with your body so stiff and sore that you needed to be lifted out of the cockpit by your groundcrew.

Doing it once earned you membership to the club. But make one mistake, or have a touch of bad luck, and you had a very good chance of ending up dead.

This book tells the little-known story of these brave men and their efforts to defeat the forces defending Japan during the final five months of World War 2. Used initially to provide fighter escort for B-29s bombing Tokyo and other cities on Japan's main island of Honshu, the Iwo Jima-based P-51 pilots enjoyed such success that they were soon called on to make low-level attacks against ground targets in preparation for the expected invasion of Japan.

On the following pages of this volume you will get to know the three Mustang-equipped Very Long Range (VLR) fighter groups of the USAAF's VII Fighter Command – the 15th, 21st and 506th FGs – and the men who made them so successful.

By any measure, the 'Sun Setters', as VII Fighter Command called itself, did a tremendous job. Between 7 April and 14 August 1945, the Mustangs flew 51 Very Long Range missions targeting mainland Japan, of which nine were aborted due to weather.

In addition, nearly 140 strikes were flown against targets in the Bonin Islands, principally on the island of Chichi Jima. In the course of those missions, Mustang pilots scored 234.5 confirmed aerial victories, plus another 219 Japanese aircraft destroyed on the ground. It would be impossible to produce an accurate tally of the ground targets damaged or destroyed by the marauding Mustang pilots, but suffice it to say they took a heavy toll on Japanese rail, road and water traffic, airfield facilities and ground emplacements.

The cost was substantial, with 131 P-51s lost and 99 pilots killed, but it is worth noting that by far the majority of losses were attributable to ground fire and bad weather. Indeed, only a handful of VLR Mustangs was shot down in air-to-air combat.

Several factors contributed to the success of VII Fighter Command's operations. Good equipment was a crucial element, and here the 'Sun Setters' shone. Their North American P-51D Mustangs were arguably the best propeller-driven fighters of World War 2, combining

1Lt William F Savidge of the 531st FS/21st FG models the 'Tokyo Club' emblem on his A-2 flying jacket (*Bill Savidge*)

speed, manoeuvrability, firepower and long range in an aeroplane that was usually ultra reliable and relatively easy to fly even when fully loaded with fuel and ammunition.

VII Fighter Command was also a highly skilled unit. Many of the pilots in the 15th and 21st FGs came to Iwo Jima with prior combat experience, and most of the rest had spent long months in training while in Hawaii. The 506th FG had just a smattering of pilots with combat experience, but many others had spent several years as training command instructors and had hundreds of flight hours in their log books. On the ground, the technicians and support personnel who worked long hours keeping the aeroplanes flying were dedicated and highly competent as well.

Meanwhile, at the far end of the 650-mile trip to Tokyo, the defending Japanese Naval Air Force (JNAF) and Japanese Army Air Force (JAAF) air units were no match for VII Fighter Command. By 1945 few veteran Japanese pilots remained alive, and their replacements graduating from truncated flight school programmes had barely enough experience to handle docile training aeroplanes, much less the high-performance fighters they were expected to fly in demanding high altitude engagments with American fighters and heavy bombers. Lacking not only flying skills but also familiarity with combat tactics and techniques, these young pilots would be lucky to survive even a single encounter with VII Fighter Command Mustangs.

As a result of this volatile combination of factors, the 'Sun Setters' were able to roam freely over Central Honshu throughout the spring and summer of 1945, creating havoc wherever they went. Their contribution to the Allies' final victory in the Pacific War was a significant one. This is their story.

Carl Molesworth
Mount Vernon, Washington
June 2006

THE LONG ROAD TO TOKYO

Around midday on 1 November 1944, air raid sirens began to wail in Tokyo. The people who did not immediately take shelter would have strained their eyes to pick out a single silver aeroplane flying high over their city. Some six miles above them, Capt Ralph D Steakley of the 3rd Photo Reconnaissance Squadron, US Army Air Force, and his crew of the aptly named Boeing B-29 Superfortress *Tokyo Rose* flew on a steady course, unhindered by Japanese interceptors or anti-aircraft fire. It was the first overflight of the Japanese capital by an American aircraft since Lt Col Jimmy Doolittle had led his daring B-25 raid against Tokyo in April 1942.

Fortunately for the citizens of Tokyo, no bombs fell from *Tokyo Rose* that day, for she was an F-13A camera ship, not a B-29 heavy bomber. But unfortunately for the people of Tokyo, the photographs taken by Capt Steakley's crew would provide valuable target intelligence for XXI Bomber Command mission planners in the recently captured Marianas Islands, some 1300 miles south of Tokyo. More photo missions followed over the next few weeks, each one adding to the Americans' knowledge of potential targets in the Tokyo area. As future events would show, the Tokyo air raid alarm of 1 November 1944 signalled the beginning of the end of the Pacific War.

Through nearly eight years of war, dating back to the first clash with Chinese troops on the Marco Polo Bridge on the outskirts of Peking in 1937, Tokyo had been spared the horrors of the war its leaders had instigated. While Japanese bombers had ravaged city after city in China and Southeast Asia, Tokyo remained virtually untouched.

Even the massive air attack against the great American naval base at Pearl Harbor on 7 December 1941, which drew the United States into the war, had only elicited in response the pinprick damage caused by Doolittle's raiders four months later. Indeed, the next raid by American bombers against Japan did not come until June 1944, when B-29s based in China attacked targets in northern Kyushu. But the logistics required to support the B-29s in China were horrific, and, in any case, the big Boeing bombers lacked the range to reach Tokyo and the other key industrial cities of central Honshu.

All that changed on 24 November 1944. After a typhoon had delayed them for a week, 111 B-29s of the 73rd BW, each laden down with two-and-a-half tons of incendiary and general purpose bombs, began taking off from Saipan at 0615 hrs for the six-hour flight to Tokyo. By the time the formation reached landfall on the coast of Japan, 17 bombers had dropped out due to mechanical problems, but the rest bore in on the Nakajima aircraft engine plant at Musashino, in northwestern Tokyo – the bombers' primary target.

The primary duty of VII Fighter Command on Iwo Jima was to provide escort for XXI Bomber Command's B-29s attacking Japan from the Marianas Islands. Here, two officers pose in front of a B-29 from the 330th BG/314th BW on the ramp at Guam. After May 1945, the need for escorts dropped considerably as enemy interceptions dwindled, so the 'Sun Setters' shifted their attention to targets on the ground (*Ed Mikes*)

Fierce winds buffeted the big bombers over Tokyo as they strained to reach their assigned altitude of 35,000 ft. As a result, only 24 aeroplanes were able to bomb the primary target, causing minimal damage to the Nakajima facilities. The rest dropped on the secondary target – dock and urban areas – with similar results. About 125 Japanese fighters intercepted the B-29s, which also encountered moderate flak, but only two of the bombers went down.

Following a small night mission on the night of 29-30 November, the 73rd BW sent another major force against the Musashino factory on 3 December. Again, high winds hampered bombing accuracy, and the target suffered little damage.

A pattern was beginning to emerge. A year earlier the USAAF brass, dominated by bomber advocates, had figured correctly that the B-29s flying at high altitude over Japan would be able to defend themselves sufficiently to hold losses to an acceptable level. But the planners had not reckoned with the effect that the wind patterns over Japan would have on bombing accuracy. Sure, the B-29s could survive over Japan at 35,000 ft, but could they bomb from up there and hit their targets? Increasingly, the answer appeared to be no.

By 20 January 1945, when Maj Gen Curtis E LeMay arrived in the Marianas Islands to assume command of XXI Bomber Command, the B-29s had flown 13 missions against major targets in Japan, but had achieved successful results only three times. Something needed to change, and change it would. First, LeMay would try low-level night attack, then, when fighter escort became available, he could get down to precision daylight raids that would finally lay waste to Japan's industrial capability.

'PINEAPPLES' AND 'YARDBIRDS'

On the morning of 6 March 1945, a P-51D Mustang took off from Isely Field, on Saipan. The pilot of the sleek fighter, Brig Gen Ernest M 'Mickey' Moore, slowly circled the island as 24 Mustangs of the 47th FS took off in pairs and found their places in formation behind him.

VII Fighter Command commanding officer Brig Gen E M 'Mickey' Moore (right) has a conversation with Ed Markham of the 47th FS. Moore, a West Pointer, was awarded the Distinguished Service Medal for 'planning and executing very long range fighter operations against the Japanese Empire' as commander of 'The Sunsetters'. Markham commanded the 47th FS during the summer of 1945 (*John Googe*)

When Brig Gen Moore was satisfied that his Mustangs were formed up properly, he turned north and began climbing, all the while scanning the sky in front of him. Soon a black dot appeared. It quickly grew into the shape of a B-29 Superfortress, the mother hen that would lead Moore and his chicks to their destination – the embattled island of Iwo Jima, some 650 miles away.

If 'Mickey' Moore was excited that morning, he had every reason to be. The 37-year-old West Pointer had been waiting more than three years to lead his pilots into combat against the Japanese, and now he was about to get the opportunity. As commanding officer of VII Fighter Command, Moore had been given the job of providing fighter escort for XXI Bomber Command B-29s that had recently commenced an intensive bombing campaign against the home islands of Japan.

Moore was highly qualified for the job. A Midwesterner, he graduated from the US Military Academy in 1931 and earned his wings at Kelly Field, Texas, the following year. His early flying career included stints as a fighter pilot flying P-12s with the 77th Pursuit Squadron and a period on detached service as an air mail pilot in his home state of Illinois. In 1936-37 Moore attended a graduate course in meteorology at the Massachusetts Institute of Technology, followed by an assignment as base weather officer at Langley Field, Virginia. Then, in the summer of 1939, he was sent to Hawaii – an assignment that would set the course for his entire experience in World War 2.

'Mickey' Moore was a major serving as assistant chief of staff for personnel in the Hawaiian Air Force (HAF) on 7 December 1941 when he watched helplessly as Japanese naval aircraft bombed and strafed American military installations in and around Pearl Harbor – the fateful attack that forced the United States into World War 2. In short order, the HAF was redesignated the Seventh Air Force, and VII Fighter Command was formed under it, with Moore assigned to serve as its executive officer.

During the early stages of the Pacific War, VII Fighter Command flew P-39s and P-40s in defence of the Hawaiian Islands. Following a period of out-of-the-way assignments, the 47th FS adopted the nickname 'Dogpatchers' and began naming its aircraft for characters in the popular comic strip 'Lil Abner'. This photograph shows Maj Norval Heath, 47th FS CO in 1943, with P-40E *MAMMY YOKUM* (*Dwayne Tabatt*)

Two years later, he was appointed commanding officer of VII Fighter Command – now nicknamed the 'Sun Setters' for the effect its pilots expected to have on the Japanese – and was promoted to his current rank.

Now, as the miles of empty ocean rolled by under the wings of his P-51, Moore had time to consider how far he and his command had come since the Pearl Harbor attack. His first two years with VII Fighter Command had involved a lot of hard work, and more than a few frustrations.

In the opening days of the war, the primary mission of the command was to provide air defence for the Hawaiian Islands in case the Japanese should attempt another air attack. With two fighter groups – the 15th and 18th – and a smattering of aircraft ranging from antiquated Boeing P-26 Peashooters to the latest model P-39Ds and P-40Es, VII Fighter Command deployed its squadrons to airfields throughout the islands and prepared for a repeat engagement with the Japanese. But the American victory at Midway in June 1942 changed the course of the war in the Pacific, and it became increasingly unlikely that the enemy would be able to strike at Hawaii again.

The focus of the Pacific war shifted south to New Guinea and then the Solomon Islands. With that, VII Fighter Command's focus shifted as well. The air defence mission remained in place, but now the main job was to put the final polish on the training of fighter pilots who were heading south to join the fighting with the Fifth and Thirteenth Air Forces.

Hundreds of pilots rotated through the fighter squadrons in Hawaii, and eventually the entire 18th FG was transferred to the Thirteenth Air Force on Guadalcanal. The 318th FG arrived in-theatre to fill the open slot left by the 18th FG's departure.

Meanwhile, VII Fighter Command deployed squadrons to such remote spots in the Central Pacific as Midway, Canton and Baker islands – all dead-end assignments where the chance of getting into action was absolutely nil.

Through it all, 'Mickey' Moore and the other leaders of the 'Sun Setters' stuck to their jobs, frustrating though it must have been to be cast in a supporting role for the main show down south. Finally, in the autumn of 1943, VII Fighter Command got its first major combat assignment – providing aerial support for the joint amphibious operation against the Gilbert Islands. Following the capture of Makin Atoll and Tarawa, the next campaign was Operation *Flintlock* – the taking of Kwajalein Atoll, in the Marshall Islands. Three VII Fighter Command squadrons (the 45th FS with P-40s, plus the 46th FS and 72nd FS with P-39s) took part in the campaigns.

Combined, the three squadrons flew more than 1100 effective sorties, including bomber escort, strafing, dive-bombing, fighter sweeps and patrols. In one escort mission on 26 January 1944, the 45th FS encountered JNAF Zeros over Maloelop Atoll and scored ten confirmed victories and two probables for no losses (see *P-40 Warhawk Aces of the Pacific* for further details). The P-39 pilots recorded several victories as well.

With the successful completion of Operation *Flintlock* in March 1944, the squadrons returned to Hawaii. Young fighter pilots who had left here six months earlier with more spirit than experience came back as blooded veterans. One such individual was Herb Henderson, whose experience was typical of the pilots who flew P-40Ns in the 45th FS in 1943-44;

'I finished pilot training on 15 March 1943 and was commissioned a second lieutenant. I got ten hours of training in the P-40E before being sent to Hawaii, where I was assigned to the 15th FG, with subsequent assignment to the 47th FS (P-40s). I transferred to the 45th FS in August 1943 and remained with the 45th through the Baker Island, Marshall Islands and Iwo campaigns.

'The Baker and Marshall islands campaigns were excellent training for the long over-water flights that were required at Iwo. They sure taught us to live "camping out". Since all of our flying was over water, we learned to trust our compass and other sparse navigation equipment. The Marshalls campaign provided the advanced training we needed to improve our skills in the dive-bombing and strafing of targets.'

The experience of pilots such as Henderson would prove to be an important factor in the future success of VII Fighter Command, because many of these men would form the leadership core of their squadrons a year later when they commenced operations over Japan.

But in the spring of 1944, as these combat veterans got themselves resettled in Hawaii, there was no way of knowing this was in their future. Nor could they know that back in Washington, D.C., military planners were already looking ahead to the strategic bombing offensive against the Japanese home islands, and the role they had in mind for VII Fighter

Command. And few, if any, of these young American pilots had ever heard of a remote island half an ocean away called Iwo Jima.

When 'Mickey' Moore assumed command of VII Fighter Command in April 1944, he had two fighter groups – the 15th and 318th, with four squadrons apiece – under his wing. Almost immediately, each of these groups gave up one squadron to the newly-forming 21st FG. In addition, VII Fighter Command was soon relieved of its responsibility to provide fighter pilots for the South Pacific. On top of that, new P-38 Lightning and P-47 Thunderbolts began arriving to replace VII Fighter Command's service-weary Airacobras and Warhawks.

It seemed clear now that the 'brass' in Washington, D.C. had plans for 'Mickey' Moore's command, and proof was not long in coming. When American forces invaded the Marianas Islands in June 1944, the 318th FG was sent to Saipan to assist in the campaign.

This left the 15th FG (led by Col James O Beckwith) and the 21st FG (under Lt Col Kenneth R Powell) in Hawaii. Both men were veteran 'Pineapples' – the term for men who had spent a long time serving in the Hawaiian Islands. To them would fall the responsibility of preparing their groups for the next assignment.

Beckwith, a Vermonter, was already an experienced pilot when he joined the USAAC in 1937. February 1941 found him offshore Hawaii aboard the aircraft carrier USS *Enterprise*, one of 31 Army pilots assigned to fly their P-36 Hawk fighters off the carrier deck for delivery to Wheeler Field, on Oahu. The pilots achieved this historic 'first' for the Army on 26 February, and stayed on to fill out the ranks of pilots in the Hawaii-based fighter squadrons. When the fighter force was expanded in October 1941, Beckwith was given command of the newly-formed 72nd FS. Two months later he watched in horror as his squadron's new P-40s were wiped out on the ground by strafing Japanese fighters during the Pearl Harbor attack.

After spending the following year leading his squadron on various deployments around the Hawaiian Islands, Beckwith was sent to New

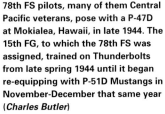

78th FS pilots, many of them Central Pacific veterans, pose with a P-47D at Mokialea, Hawaii, in late 1944. The 15th FG, to which the 78th FS was assigned, trained on Thunderbolts from late spring 1944 until it began re-equipping with P-51D Mustangs in November-December that same year (*Charles Butler*)

2Lt Doyle Brooks of the 78th FS flew P-47D *BUTTON* in Hawaii during 1944. After more than two years flying P-40s, the pilots of the 15th FG were very happy to transition to the powerful Thunderbolt. Note the gaudy black/yellow/black bands and 'Bushmasters' squadron badge on the cowling (*Doyle Brooks*)

Guinea in January 1943 to study the combat techniques that V Fighter Command was using successfully against the Japanese in the Southwest Pacific. He flew five combat missions during his stay and then returned to Hawaii. In September 1943 Beckwith was elevated to command of the 15th FG.

His three fighter squadrons – the 45th, 47th and 78th FSs – were equipped with P-47D Thunderbolts in 1944. As we have seen, the 45th had by far the most combat experience of the three. In fact, its commanding officer, Maj Gilmer L 'Buck' Snipes, had scored the unit's first aerial victory of the war in October 1943, and 14 other squadron pilots had flown with him during the Marshalls campaign. The 78th FS spent January through to April 1943 on Midway Island, but saw no action there beyond friendly gunnery contests against the Marine Corps, which also had forces occupying the island.

Among the 78th FS's four combat veterans were the CO, Maj James M Vande Hey, who had scored two confirmed victories in the Marshalls, and Capt Robert W 'Todd' Moore, who had one victory to his credit.

The 47th FS, meanwhile, had been the top-scoring squadron on 7 December 1941 with seven confirmed victories, but had remained in the Hawaiian Islands throughout the war. The 47th had christened itself the 'Dogpatch' squadron because the out-of-the-way airfields it had inhabited reminded the men of the home of comic strip character 'Li'l Abner.' As far as can be determined, its only combat veteran was 1Lt Dick Hintermeier.

Ken Powell assumed command of the 21st FG when the group was activated at Bellows Field on 21 April 1944, after serving under Beckwith in the 15th FG prior to that. A native of Oregon, he grew up in Tacoma, Washington, and got his first taste of military life in the Reserve Officer Training Corps while a student at Washington State College (now a university). On graduating from college in 1938, Powell joined the Army as an infantry officer and served in that capacity until the autumn of 1939, when he entered flight training. Powell graduated from Kelly Field in flying class 40D and was sent to Hawaii, where he joined the 78th FS in September 1940.

The 531st FS began life as a dive-bombing unit, flying the A-24 (the USAAF's version of the Navy SBD Dauntless) during the Central Pacific campaign. Upon arriving in Hawaii in the spring of 1944, the squadron was assigned to the newly-formed 21st FG and issued with Airacobras, among them P-39D-1 41-38288 (*John Galbraith*)

Like the other pilots in his squadron, Powell had no opportunity to get airborne during the Japanese attack on 7 December 1941. He transferred to the 46th FS as squadron commander in November 1942 and led the unit to remote Canton Island the following spring. Powell was appointed deputy CO of the 15th FG in April 1943, and held that post until he was assigned to organise the 21st FG a year later.

All three of Powell's squadrons in the 21st FG had seen combat in the Central Pacific during 1943 and early 1944, and all three contained combat veterans on their pilot rosters. The 46th and 72nd FSs had flown P-39s, but the 531st had been a fighter-bomber squadron, equipped with Douglas A-24 Banshees – the Army version of the Navy's famous SBD Dauntless dive-bomber. With its A-24 flight crews replaced by fighter pilots, the 531st FS flew P-39s with the 46th and 72nd FSs until midsummer 1944, when all three squadrons of the 21st FG received new P-38 Lightnings.

This was a period of transition for VII Fighter Command. Many of the old 'Pineapple' pilots were sent back to the US for training, leave or reassignment, while replacement pilots – called 'Yardbirds' by the old hands – arrived to fill the open slots. Combat veterans were transferred among the squadrons to try to create a balance of experience. As the year progressed, the training intensified.

Two of the many 'Yardbirds' who joined the 15th FG from the USA during this period were Flt Off Bert Combs and 2Lt Bob Kriss. The former recalled;

'My prior military experience consisted entirely of aviation cadet and post-cadet flight training in P-40s and P-47s. I joined the 15th FG in late October 1944 at Bellows Field, Hawaii. There were 12 of us fresh from the P-47 Replacement Training Unit at Abilene, Texas. We received a

very "warm" welcome from the 15th FG CO, Col Jim Beckwith, who told us we were unwanted and unwelcome as we had no combat experience, but that they would make the most of it and do something with us. What a confidence-builder.'

Kriss, who arrived in Hawaii with Combs and was assigned to the 47th FS, recalled;

'Whatever we had learned about flying to this point was kindergarten. These people flew "balls-to-the-wall" all the time, and expected the same from us "Yardbirds". One day, Ed Markham, who was 47th ops officer at the time, had me flying his wing. I got as close as I felt was prudent and he kept motioning me closer. Just about the time I could read the second hand on his wristwatch, he turned into me! Lordy, the brakes didn't work and none of the controls were designed for the manoeuvre I had in mind. Eyes closed and bowels locked, I survived, and found myself in a fairly reasonable position on Ed's wing. I was learning how to take care of myself and how to make myself useful no matter what the situation called for.'

After long months of training, the 15th FG was alerted for deployment to a combat area. Morale skyrocketed as the men packed in anticipation of joining the force being assembled for the impending invasion of the Caroline Islands. Col Beckwith departed with his staff for the western Pacific, but two weeks later he returned with the bad news that the invasion had been cancelled. The Allies would be taking the Philippines instead, and the Fifth and Thirteenth Air Forces had all the fighters they needed to do that job. Deeply disappointed, the men of the 15th FG went back to their mundane daily routines.

November 1944 brought more turmoil, when the 21st FG was given the unwelcome task of flying 36 of its Lightnings across the Pacific to Saipan. Here, the group would turn its near-new fighters over to the 318th FG for use on long-range escort missions against the bypassed Japanese stronghold at Truk. Twenty-four of the 21st FG pilots swapped into the 318th FG with their aeroplanes, but the rest returned to Oahu, and more dull duty.

The 21st FG traded its P-39s for P-38Js (this one is a 72nd FS machine) in mid-1944 and began training for very long range operations. Later that year, many of these aircraft, and their pilots, were transferred to the 318th FG on Saipan to give the group the long-range capability that its P-47Ds could not (*Lloyd Hild*)

On a brighter note, 'Mickey' Moore returned from a trip to England, where he had gone in September to confer with Eighth Air Force commanders about long-range escort operations. In particular, Moore needed to learn all he could about the newest fighter in the USAAF arsenal, the North American P-51 Mustang, which the 8th AF had been operating with great success over occupied Europe since December 1943.

The reason for Moore's trip to England became evident soon after his return to Hawaii, when the first shipment of brand new North American P-51D-20 Mustangs was delivered to Hickam Air Depot on Oahu. At about the same time, VII Fighter Command advised its units to prepare to ship out for a combat zone. The pace of life picked up, for the introduction of a new aircraft into the squadrons meant nearly everyone – from the pilots and crew chiefs to the armourers, supply people and more – needed to familiarise themselves with the Mustang.

George Brown, assistant 21st FG operations officer, and a veteran of Makin operations with the 46th FS, recalled this period vividly;

'We flew P-38s until December 1944, when we received our new P-51 Mustangs. We only had about six weeks to get to know the aeroplane. I did a lot of testing – fuel consumption, with five trips between Kauai and Hawaii nonstop, and testing the new homing radio. Our radios were four-

VII Fighter Command squadrons wasted no time in decorating their new fighters when they re-equipped with P-51Ds in November-December 1944. Here, a crewman applies the 'Bushmasters' emblem on a new 78th FS Mustang. Each squadron had distinctive markings to help pilots distinguish one unit from another in the air (*Tom Ivie*)

channel transmitter-receivers, with an IFF (Identification, Friend or Foe) transmitter, plus a homing receiver to pick up the B-29 navigator aeroplanes that would lead us across the Pacific to our targets and then back home once again.

'The P-51D had six 0.50-cal Browning machine guns mounted in the wings. It had underwing racks to carry either bombs or extra drop tanks. It was a fantastic flying machine. It had a 1695 hp Packard-Merlin engine that only burned 40 gallons per hour on a long-range mission.'

The experience of the 531st FS/21st FG during this period was typical of all the squadrons. Seven P-51Ds were delivered to the 531st in December 1944, and they were put to work immediately as the 40 pilots in the squadron checked out in them, logging from three to 13.5 hours apiece in the new aeroplanes. At the same time, the engineering department was hard at work installing IFF units in the fighters. To do this, they first moved the battery from its factory location under the canopy to a spot in the engine compartment, and then mounted the IFF under the canopy. Another key task was painting group and squadron markings on the aeroplanes.

More P-51Ds arrived in January, allowing the 531st to compile 1121 hours of Mustang flight time during the month. Included in the flight schedule were four practice escort missions carried out with B-25 Mitchells of the 41st BG. Perhaps the most exciting event came on 31 January 1945, though few men of the squadron actually witnessed it. Maj Sam Hudson, 531st CO, and Maj DeWitt Spain from group headquarters embarked in an aircraft carrier, along with two P-51s, and were taken about five miles out to sea. From there, the two pilots made

Eighty-two Mustangs of the 15th FG were shipped to the Marianas Islands from Hawaii aboard the aircraft carrier USS *Sitkoh Bay* in early February 1945. Here, P-51D-20 44-63395 *Daisy Mae* of the 47th FS is craned off the carrier and barged ashore at Guam. From there, the aeroplanes were flown to Tinian and then on to Iwo Jima, when the 811th Aviation Engineer Battalion completed repairs to Airfield No 1, North Field, on 6-7 March (*Tom Ivie*)

catapult take-offs from the carrier deck and flew back to their base at Bellows Field.

The 531st was now declared on mobile status, and the men began packing their gear and belongings. The squadron history observed, 'Many of the ground personnel were with the 531st at Makin with the A-24s, which showed excellent results'. Another indication that VII Fighter Command would be moving out soon was the change of address to APO 86, wherever that was!

The squadrons of the two groups reorganised themselves into air and ground echelons in preparation for the move. The 15th FG loaded its 82 P-51s aboard the escort carrier USS *Sitkoh Bay* at Ford Island, in Pearl Harbor, and cast off for the high seas on 2 February, bound for Guam. The 21st FG did likewise with USS *Hollandia* a week later. At Guam, the P-51s were lifted off the carrier decks by cranes, relieving the pilots of the need to fly their aeroplanes off the ships. The 15th FG flew its fighters from Guam to Saipan on 14 February, and the 21st headed to Tinian one week later.

Meanwhile, the ground echelons of both groups had boarded liberty ships for their treks west. The 15th FG ground echelon left Hawaii on 27 January and arrived offshore a small island in the Volcano group, about 650 miles south of Tokyo, about three weeks later. The island was called Iwo Jima.

ASSAULT ON IWO JIMA

One look at a map is all it takes to understand why a huge American invasion fleet carrying 30,000 battle-ready US Marines was standing off the coast of Iwo Jima on the morning 19 February 1945. For nearly a year, military planners in Washington, D.C. had been focused on Iwo Jima as a

The 21st FG was a week behind the 15th FG leaving Pearl Harbor, where P-51D-20 44-63390 of the 46th FS was loaded aboard the escort carrier USS *Hollandia* with a set of drop tanks attached. The group flew combat air patrols on Tinian for several weeks before moving up to Iwo Jima's Central Field on 22 March 1945 (*Tom Ivie*)

19

key element in their strategy to take the air war in the Pacific directly to the Japanese home islands. In Allied hands, this pin-prick of land in the vast ocean could prove invaluable during the upcoming strategic bombing campaign against Japan. It could provide not only a haven for damaged and fuel-starved B-29s returning to their bases farther south, but also a base for fighters that would provide protection for the big bombers over their target areas.

Conversely, Japanese strategists had recognised the value of the island as a bulwark in the defence of Japan. In mid-1944, Japanese bombers and fighters based on Iwo Jima had flown numerous missions opposing the Allies' invasion of the Marianas. At that time, the small island was little more than a stationary Japanese aircraft carrier, with two airfields defended by a just handful of troops.

Legendary JNAF fighter ace Saburo Sakai, arriving for duty on Iwo Jima in June 1944, was shocked to see the island's meagre defences, and was further surprised that the Americans did not invade it immediately after securing their positions in the Marianas. Instead, the Americans focused next on the invasion of the Philippines, giving the Japanese seven valuable months to build up their defences on Iwo Jima.

And build up they did. By February 1945 there were approximately 23,000 Japanese troops dug in on the island. They had constructed a web of interlocking strongholds connected by caves from one end of the eight-square-mile island to the other, with hundreds of steel-reinforced concrete blockhouses, pillboxes and communications centres. Camouflaged artillery positions and machine-gun nests covered every approach to the

Iwo Jima was not much to look at, even from the air. Mount Suribachi, in the foreground, with South Field just beyond, was an extinct volcano at the south end of the island, which measured about six miles long and two miles wide (*Ed Linfante*)

island, and the black sand beaches were sown with mines. Mt Suribachi, an extinct volcano at the southern end of the island, was honeycombed with caves connecting gun emplacements and observation posts.

American naval forces began pounding Iwo Jima with a steady barrage of bombs and heavy artillery in early December 1944. The island's airfields were quickly rendered useless, but the hardened positions suffered hardly a scratch in the 74-day assault. Thus, when the Marines went ashore on 19 February, they were in for one of the bloodiest fights of the entire Pacific War.

Among those in the invasion fleet were the men in the ground echelon of the 15th FG embarked in the transport ships *Berrien* and *Lenawee*. Their job would be to go ashore as soon as practicable to prepare the airfield called Motoyama No 1 for the arrival of the group's P-51s. That was not possible until D-Day plus six. Two junior pilots of the 47th FS within the ground echelon were Bob Kriss and John Fitzgerald. The latter recalled;

'We went ashore in two LCIs (landing craft infantry). The beach where we landed was a mess with destroyed LCIs and dead and wounded Marines. I believe we went in along with Marines of the 3rd Division, which was the back-up division behind the 4th and 5th. The 3rd was called on to go in early because of the heavy casualties suffered in the initial assault.

'We went in at about noon as I recall, and immediately started digging two-man foxholes maybe 100 ft up from the water's edge. Somehow or other we got some sand bags, because the black sand fell right back into the hole we were digging. Fellow pilot Merlin Kinsey and I dug a hole three feet deep and covered it with two tent tarps. We crawled in there as it got dark and stayed put, even though the Navy threw up star shells all night,

The ground echelon of the 15th FG landed on Iwo Jima on 25 February 1945, less than a week after the Marines invaded the island. The men set up a rudimentary air base, stocked with fuel, ammunition and bombs, for the group's aircraft (*John Googe*)

as the Japs would infiltrate our lines after dark. The Marines had 0.30-cal machine guns set up around the area, and they fired at every sound and movement all night long.'

Kriss had a similar experience;

'The Marines hit the beach on 19 February while we cruised offshore, watching the bombardment. How anything or anybody could have survived it is beyond comprehension. Six days later the Navy kicked us off its boat. We landed on the northwest side of the bay as far away from Suribachi as possible to protect the landing craft, I suppose. Then the powers that be marched us back into the shadow of Suribachi, pointed to the hillside and told us to dig in.

'I was paired with John Scanlan (later killed in action). Each of us had a digging tool and one half of a pup tent. Digging in the black sand was not easy, however, for every shovelful you threw out of the hole, two more fell back in. By dark, John and I had a hole about three feet deep and twenty feet around. We pitched our pup tent in the middle of the excavation and went to sleep.

'Some fool who couldn't stand the peace and quiet fired a round into Suribachi and the Japs got even. They dropped a few knee mortars and fired some light machine-gun rounds into the area. John and I managed to dig our hole a little deeper!

'After a week or so we left the beach and dug in at the northern end of Motoyama No 1 airfield. We spent most of our time setting up shop for maintenance, operations, parts etc., so as to be functional when the aircraft came in from Saipan.'

Fellow 'Yardbird' pilot Joe Wanamaker of the 45th FS gave this account;

'We came ashore on the day the flag went up on Suribachi. Eyeball view, smell and sound of what war is like? No way I can describe it, but it does

Wreckage from the fighting was strewn all over the island when VII Fighter Command first arrived on Iwo Jima. This was a Japanese Type 95 light tank that ran afoul of the invading Marines' firepower. Developed to meet the requirements of the Japanese Army in the early 1930s, the Type 95 was a useful vehicle in China, but did not survive long when facing the M4 Sherman or American anti-tank equipment (*Ed Linfante*)

leave a lasting impression on you. Since the island was not yet secured, our assigned area near the airstrip was still under fire, so the Marines were kind enough to let us dig our foxholes in their artillery area. We were really prepared for the ground action – pistols and carbines with limited ammo, gas mask, tarp, blanket, canteen and two boxes of K-rations.

'The overall master plan was slightly off schedule. The island was supposed to be secured before we went ashore, but it was about ten days before we moved to our assigned area on the airstrip. At this time we dug better foxholes and scrounged boxes and other materials to hold back the sand. Much later we were issued with floored tents and finally Quonset huts.'

LEARNING THE ROPES

The Marine Corps' epic struggle to wrest control of Iwo Jima from its Japanese defenders is the stuff of legend. As the Marines came ashore on 19 February they found themselves bogged down in the island's loose

This map of Iwo Jima was produced by the US Navy in the final weeks of World War 2. The four runways which turned the island into an 'unsinkable aircraft carrier' are clearly marked

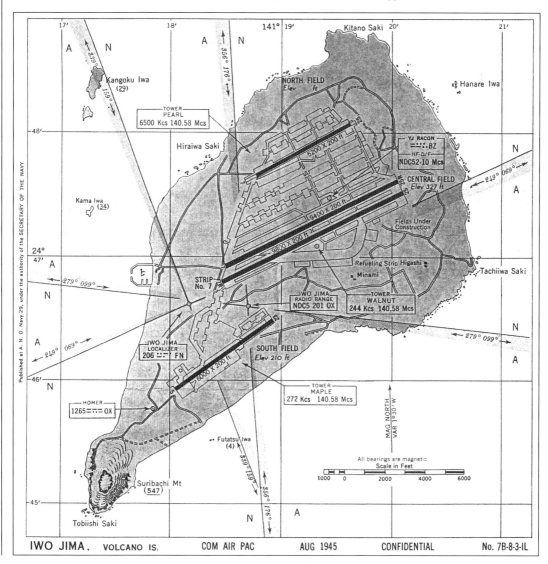

Col James O Beckwith, commanding officer of the 15th FG, leads the 45th and 78th FSs to Iwo Jima on 10 March. Beckwith is flying the P-51D at upper left, 44-63423 *Squirt*, which boasted 47th FS markings. The fighter was subsequently destroyed on Iwo Jima in late April when a B-29 ran into it during a crash-landing (*Tom Ivie*)

volcanic ash and under fire from enemy positions they could not see. In the first few hours of the battle they were able to establish a beachhead on the southeast coast that was a mere 4500 yards long and 500 yards deep. From there they began their bloody advance up the rocky hillsides of the plateau.

In the first 48 hours, fighting without sleep and often in pouring rain, the Marines suffered some 3650 casualties. But they continued to push forward. By the end of the first week they had captured both airfields and were clearing out the Japanese defenders on 546 ft-high Mount Suribachi cave by cave and pillbox by pillbox. With no hope of reinforcement or withdrawal, the Japanese fought back fiercely.

It was during this period that Associated Press photographer Joe Rosenthal snapped his famous picture of the American flag-raising atop Suribachi, but the fighting for the island continued for another three weeks before the island was declared secured. The cost in human lives was enormous. The Marines would suffer 20,196 casualties, including 4189 men killed. Even that number paled when compared to the losses of the Japanese – of nearly 23,000 defenders, only about 200 were taken prisoner. The rest perished.

Often working while under fire, the men of the 811th Aviation Engineer Battalion meanwhile had completed their work of clearing wreckage and patching the cratered runway at Airfield No 1, which was soon to be called South Field. Working alongside the engineers, the ground echelon of the 15th FG had set up a rudimentary air base, stocked with fuel, ammunition and bombs for the group's aircraft.

On 6 March the airfield was declared ready for operations, and Brig Gen 'Mickey' Moore led his 25 Mustangs of the 47th FS to the embattled island that same day. Col Jim Beckwith followed from Saipan on 7 March, with the 45th and 78th FSs in tow. Charles Butler was one of the 78th FS pilots who made the flight;

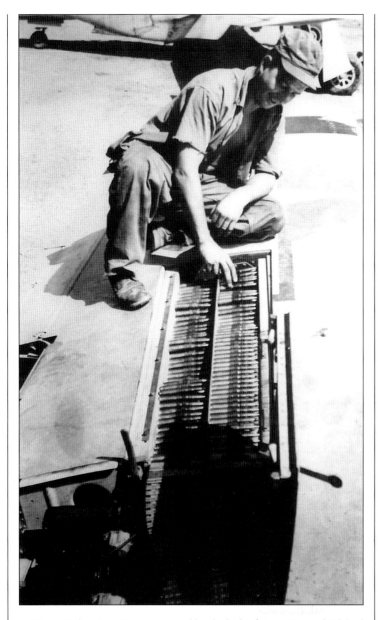

All P-51D Mustangs flown by VII Fighter Command were fitted with six 0.50-cal M-2 machine guns (three in each wing), and carried 1000 rounds of ammunition. Here, a 72nd FS armourer carefully loads ammunition into the left wing compartment of a Mustang (*Bob Sterritt*)

'On arrival on Iwo, I was surprised by the lack of vegetation, which had been destroyed by air bombing, heavy offshore naval fire, ground fire and the creation of dug-outs, built mostly by the Japs. Many dead Japs had been quickly buried and only partially covered, and some were still exposed.'

Bob Scamara, a junior pilot in the 47th FS, was in the secondary group of pilots who flew from Saipan to Iwo Jima aboard a C-46 Commando transport. His first few days on Iwo left a lasting impression;

'By then the Marines had taken about half of Iwo, with severe casualties, poor guys. We ended up in fox holes in our assigned area. We could watch the big guns lobbing shells over our heads into Jap lines. The guns were still at the southern end of the island. The frontline was only a couple of miles away. We could see their shells in flight over our heads, they were going so slow. And at night they kept the island lit up with flares, just like daylight.'

Action started almost immediately for the 15th FG Mustang pilots, when the Marines sent a message on 8 March requesting an air strike against particularly stubborn enemy positions on the northern coast. Capt John Piper, popular CO of the 47th FS, led two flights of P-51s aloft and made radio contact with a Marine ground coordinator, who directed him to the target using points on a grid map. The eight Mustangs duly strafed the area with 0.50-cal machine gun fire.

After the first pass, the coordinator urged Piper to come closer to the Marine frontlines, which were marked with yellow panels. Piper could not spot the panels, but adjusted his next pass in their supposed direction. Again and again the coordinator requested him to move closer, and the leading Mustang pilot complied, each time fearing his aeroplanes would overshoot the line and hit the Marines. But by the time the Mustangs had expended all their ammunition, apparently they were right on the mark. The Marines later complimented Piper's flight, calling the mission the best job of close air support they had seen in two weeks.

That night, P-61 Black Widows of the 548th Night Fighter Squadron (NFS), also recently arrived on the airfield to defend Iwo Jima from nocturnal Japanese air attacks, flew their first two sorties. They made radar contact with two bogies before losing them due to bad atmospheric conditions.

Col Beckwith got his first crack at the enemy on 9 March, leading one of three 45th FS missions in support of the Marines on Iwo. The 45th FS also sent eight-aeroplane flights to attack Kangoku and Kama islands, which stood close off the west coast of Iwo, and may have been occupied. It was the turn of the 78th FS on 10 March, and squadron CO Maj Jim Vande Hey made the most of it by flying three of the squadron's 45 sorties that day. The 10th also saw the 15th FG suffer its first battle damage,

The waters off the west coast of the island remained full of vessels for months after the invasion, as can be seen in this photograph taken from atop Mt Suribachi (*Bert Combs*)

when 2Lt Gordon H Scott's Mustang was hit in the tail section by ground fire. Scott managed to land his aeroplane safely, however. By this time the Marines had split the Japanese forces on the island, making the battle lines so close to one another that close-air-support missions were no longer feasible.

Now the Mustangs were ready to take the next step – an overwater flight to attack Japanese positions in the Bonin Islands. Located about 150 miles north of Iwo Jima, the Bonins had been a territory of Japan since the 1870s. One of the islands, Chichi Jima, featured an excellent harbour, and might have been considered for invasion instead of Iwo Jima except for the fact that its mountainous terrain allowed room for just one small airfield. Nevertheless, Chichi Jima served as an important watching and listening post, its radio station providing early warning of B-29 raids proceeding north from the Marianas toward Japan. Its Susaki Airfield was also used on occasion as a staging point for Japanese night bombers on their way to attack Iwo Jima from Japan.

Raids by US Navy aircraft, beginning in June 1944, had eliminated Chichi's fighters, but the island was strongly defended by some 14,000 Japanese troops and fairly bristled with anti-aircraft guns. In addition, Chichi had developed a nasty reputation among American flyers, who had heard rumours that downed flyers captured on the island were likely to be executed rather than being held as prisoners of war. In fact, the 'word' was that if you went down in Chichi you could expect to be clubbed, bayoneted and have your head chopped off by a samurai sword. Since rations were tight on the island, there was a good chance that your body would be cut up and tossed into the cook pot to flavour the evening's stew. Sadly, investigations after the war proved these rumours to be true.

So it was with high spirits, tempered by natural trepidation, that 17 Mustang pilots took off from Airfield No 1 on Iwo Jima just after 0900 hrs on 11 March 1945 and headed north toward Chichi Jima. The pilots were all drawn from the 47th FS save two – Col Beckwith leading 'Red Flight' and Brig Gen Moore, who tagged along to observe the attack while answering to the call sign 'Chieftain One'.

Flying in clear weather, the formation climbed to 10,000 ft and throttled back to a cruising speed of 200 mph. As would become common practice in the months to come, they passed a Navy PBY Catalina 'dumbo' rescue aeroplane about halfway to the target. The 'dumbo's' job was to come to the

The 47th FS flew the first combat mission on Iwo Jima, providing close air support on 8 March 1945 for Marines that were mopping up the last of the organised Japanese resistance on the island. Next came strikes against Chichi Jima, in the Bonin Islands, starting 11 March. Here, bombed-up P-51s of 47th FS taxi for take-off on early mission to Chichi (*Tom Ivie*)

aid of any fighter pilot who might need to parachute into the sea due to battle damage or mechanical failure. Similarly, they passed a Navy destroyer that was positioned to pick up any downed fliers. Soon, Capt Ray L Obenshain Jr, 'Blue Flight' leader, spotted Chichi Jima off to his right and called it in. Brig Gen Moore stationed himself about a mile southwest of Susaki Airfield, where he would be in position to observe the attacks on the base, and the nearby harbour.

Col Beckwith, using call sign 'Invader One', led the remaining 16 Mustangs, each carrying two 500-lb bombs, across the island to a point southeast of the airfield, where they could attack it from out of the sun. Four parked aeroplanes, one lacking a tail, came into view after Beckwith pushed over in his dive from 10,000 ft.

With 1Lts Fred T Grover, Frank L Ayres and Jule C Mitchell Jr behind him, Beckwith led 'Red Flight' down in elements toward two of the parked aeroplanes on the western side of the field and released bombs at 4,000 ft. Six of the eight bombs hit in the target area as 'Red Flight' continued its dive across the airfield and strafed the other two aeroplanes on the far side, before heading out to sea through the harbour entrance. Beckwith pulled up to 3000 ft about three miles offshore and circled while the other three flights made their attacks. He observed black puffs of flak at 2000 ft, but no one was hit.

By the time Capt Obenshain's 'Blue Flight', including Capt Theon E 'Ed' Markham and 1Lts Charles J Cameron and Joseph P Brunette, made its attack, the flak defences on Susaki Airfield had begun firing. After dropping their bombs at 2500 ft, Obenshain and Cameron flew out to join 'Red Flight', while Markham and Brunette proceeded north across the harbour to take a look at Omura town, before also joining up with the rest of the formation.

Chichi Jima, about 150 miles north of Iwo Jima, was attacked repeatedly by VII Fighter Command, as it remained occupied by the Japanese throughout the war. Despite being repeatedly attacked, the radio station tower on the island's Mt Asahi remained standing, as this photograph, taken shortly after Japan capitulated, clearly shows (*John Googe*)

Next came 'Green Flight', led by Capt Lawrence T Pepin. He and his pilots – Capt Walter H 'Sam' Powell and 1Lts Eurich L Bright and Henry C Ryniker – had a hard time picking up any specific target on the airfield because of the heavy smoke and dust kicked up by the previous attacks. They released their bombs at 5000 ft and then proceeded out to the join-up point.

'Yellow Flight', with Capt Piper leading, skipped the airfield in favour of attacking shipping in the harbour off Shiomi Point. Leading Capt Robert R Down and 1Lts Oliver E O'Mara Jr and Charles E Jennings from northeast of the harbour, Capt Piper headed for a group of about 16 small vessels and let go of his bombs. The others followed, and the flight scored one direct hit, two probable hits and the rest near-misses. The Mustangs strafed the seaplane base, noting heavy flak, before also heading to the rendezvous point.

With his Mustangs reformed, Beckwith flew south toward the neighbouring island of Haha Jima, which was also known to be defended. Arriving over the island at about 1030 hrs, the formation dove down from 4000 ft in a series of strafing runs on the town of Kitmura. They then attacked the weather station and a warehouse at Okimura. Flak was heavy, particularly at Okimura, and the P-51s flown by Obenshain and Ayres both sustained damage. But the radio station was left smoking.

Continuing south after the pass over Haha, Beckwith picked up a homing vector from the rescue destroyer and headed toward it. Once overhead the vessel he was given a second vector back to Iwo Jima. 'Mickey' Moore, meanwhile, had followed the formation to Haha Jima, but arrived there too late to observe the attacks and proceeded back to Iwo Jima on his own. All aeroplanes were back on the ground at Airfield No 1 by 1115 hrs.

The remarks portion of the 47th FS mission report for 11 March was short and to the point;

'Excellent mission. Towns in too good condition to satisfy "Invader One". Perfect performance of aeroplanes. Good weather and communications. Briefing good'.

Col Beckwith went back to the Bonin Islands for more action on 12 March, leading the 45th FS on a strike against Haha Jima. Then on 13 March he led the 78th FS on its first strike against Chichi. After this, operations were conducted almost daily over the Bonins, weather permitting.

Through the Iwo close-air support missions and the first strikes against the Bonins, the 15th FG had yet to lose a pilot. Everyone knew this could not last, and indeed it did not. 1Lt Beaver A Kinsel of the 45th FS, who was a combat veteran of nine missions during the Central Pacific campaign, went up for a combat air patrol on 17 March and vanished when the flight briefly entered some clouds. He has the sad distinction of being the first of 99 P-51 'Sun Setter' pilots who would lose their lives flying from Iwo during the course of the war.

The first loss to enemy action occurred nine days after Kinsel disappeared, when 2Lt John R Shuler of the 47th FS was hit by ground fire while strafing the radar tower at Chichi Jima. He nursed his P-51 about ten miles out to sea, bailed out and was seen to land in the water. However, when the 'dumbo' arrived on the scene about 15 minutes later,

Maj Paul Imig, 72nd FS CO, poses with his P-51D 44-63733 *Dede Lou*. After long service in VII Fighter Command, Imig finally reached his goal of flying a combat mission over Japan, prior to rotating back to the US. 44-63733 went on to complete 26 missions with just one abort (for a radio problem), thus compiling the best service record of any P-51 in the squadron (*Walter Foster*)

there was nothing to be found except Shuler's empty life vest floating in the dye-stained water.

NIGHT TERRORS

When the 15th FG arrived at Airfield No 1, the engineers turned their attention to Motoyama No 2, in the centre of the island. For 16 days they worked to make the strip ready for operations, and then on 22 March the sky filled with the roar of 20 yellow-banded P-51s of the 72nd FS/21st FG as they circled to land after the long flight from Tinian. The 21st's remaining two squadrons followed two days later, landing at 1300 hrs.

Now 'Mickey' Moore had two complete P-51 fighter groups under his command – a big enough force to provide meaningful escort protection to the B-29 formations that were continuing to pound Tokyo and other target in Central Honshu. The newly arrived 21st FG was similar in make-up to the 15th, with a mixture of veteran pilots in the leadership roles and younger 'Yardbirds' filling out the rosters. In particular, Col Powell had three strong 'Pineapples' commanding his squadrons.

Maj Fred A Shirley, CO of the 46th FS, had flown 16 missions and earned a Distinguished Flying Cross with the 45th FS in the Central Pacific. The 72nd FS CO, Maj Paul W Imig, had flown P-39s in the squadron at Canton Island, and once offered to take a reduction in rank if he could get a combat assignment in V Fighter Command. When the offer

P-51Ds of the 531st FS sit on the
flightline, probably at Tinian, in
March 1945 as their pilots await
orders to move up to Iwo Jima.
On 30 March, after arriving at Iwo's
Central Field, Mustang 44-43912
MISS JACKIE was wrecked by 1Lt
Robert H Moody when he got caught
in a crosswind and ground-looped. It
was duly transferred to the local air
service group and stripped for parts
(*Tom Ivie*)

was rejected, he agreed to stay on in the 72nd FS in the hopes that he would eventually get to see the famous Mt Fuji, near Tokyo, from the cockpit of a fighter. Maj John S 'Sam' Hudson was the popular commander of the 531st FS, but was destined not to experience aerial combat over Japan.

George Brown, assistant group operations officer, was one of the first members of the 21st FG to arrive on Iwo Jima, and his initial impression of the place was anything but positive;

'I preceded the group and flew to Iwo in a C-46 to get things ready. There was only one way to describe Iwo Jima – it was the asshole of creation. It is a volcanic island that is still covered with volcanic ash. Well water comes out hot and has sulphur in it. It was difficult to keep a tent up in the wind because the stakes would pull out of the ash. Iwo was difficult! They were building the runway while we were operating. It was a clay surface with no asphalt.'

The 21st FG's squadrons went right to work flying combat air patrols, even though the pilots had to service their own aeroplanes for the first few days before the groundcrews arrived from Tinian. In their off time, the pilots began exploring the island, despite the fact that sporadic barks of gunfire in the distance served as a reminder that Japanese troops were still holed up in caves and tunnels throughout the island. When Maj Imig learned that some of his 72nd FS pilots had been poking around up near the frontlines, he ordered an end to their escapades. Shortly thereafter, his order would become unnecessary.

Maj Lloyd A Whitley, operations officer of the 531st FS, woke up long before sunrise on 26 March 1945. He was scheduled to lead a flight in the squadron's first strike on Chichi Jima later that morning and wanted to be sure all was in readiness. Whitley was a popular figure in the squadron,

31

The first few days on Iwo were very busy ones for the personnel of the 21st FG, as they went about setting up operations on Central Field. Walter Foster, message centre chief of the 72nd FS, recalls pulling guard duty in holes dug alongside a road that the Seabees were building. 'They worked around the clock, and those GI trucks kept you alert', he recalled (*Walter Foster*)

On the night of 26 March 1945, an estimated 300 Japanese soldiers attacked the 21st FG tent area at Central Field. In the ensuing action, the 21st FG lost 14 men killed and 50 wounded, including group commander Col Ken Powell. But the raid was the last gasp for the Japanese defenders on Iwo Jima, as nearly all were killed. (*Ted Perritt*)

and many pilots had been in attendance when he married Navy nurse Ens Dorothy L Main in Hawaii on 25 January. When Whitley finished his work in the operations tent at about 0515 hrs, he began walking toward a truck about 30 yards distant, where his best man and buddy, fellow 531st pilot Capt William Benton, waited with the alert crew to drive them to the flightline. It was still quite dark, and the men could not help but notice the sporadic gunfire and explosions that had started at about 0400 hrs.

What they did not know was that the Japanese had organised about 300 soldiers to stage a night raid against Airfield No 2. Sleeping in tents in a bivouac area on the north side of the field were the officers of the 21st FG and the just-arrived 549th NFS, plus an Army unit of African-American labourers who had just been posted to Iwo to take over clean-up efforts on the island.

As Maj Whitley climbed into Benton's truck, they noticed a sharp increase in the intensity of the gunfire and then saw a number of shadowy figures running through the area. Suddenly, a hail of gunfire slammed into the vehicle. The occupants of the truck quickly bailed out and took cover underneath it, as well as beneath several Jeeps that happened to be parked nearby.

Only one of the alert crew was armed, but his gun quickly jammed, leaving the men defenceless until Whitley grabbed a carbine from a truck that pulled up next to them and returned fire. The Americans remained pinned down until relief arrived at about 0700 hrs, but at some point in the fighting Whitley had been hit in the neck by a Japanese bullet and died instantly.

Meanwhile, confusion reigned in the tent area, where most men had been sleeping when the attack began.

'We were caught barefoot and in our underwear', Jim Van Nada of the 72nd FS told the audience during a 2003 panel discussion at the Museum of Flight in Seattle. Van Nada, who was wounded by grenade fragments in the attack, was sent to Hawaii to recuperate and would return to Iwo in May to assume command of the squadron.

Fellow 72nd FS pilot 1Lt Horace Brandenberger recalled the morning this way;

'We were awakened by gunfire, thinking the Marines were trying to make our stay appear more like combat. We quickly realised there were Japs all around. As we dug into the ashy ground in our tent with our helmets, a buddy crawled in shot up and bleeding. The Marines arrived and called out to evacuate the area. I lifted the centre pole of our tent so we could get our wounded buddy out. After it was all over, I couldn't lift the pole!'

1Lt James W 'Bill' Bradbury of the 72nd FS had just arrived on Iwo the previous day, and he was assigned to a tent whose other occupants included two ex-Royal Air Force pilots;

Blue-striped P-51Ds of the 46th FS taxi into their parking positions on the line at Central Airfield. 44-63916 at left carried the name *ELAINE* on the nose, but its regular pilot is unknown. The 21st FG began flying local patrols around Iwo Jima immediately after arriving on the island in March 1945 (*Tom Ivie*)

'About 0500 hrs I was awakened by explosions. The first RAF pilot was dressed and out into the darkness. I was almost into my flying suit and shoes and halfway toward the tent flap when the second RAF pilot (1Lt Burton Bourelle of the 531st FS) started out the door, but was blown back by a grenade. I changed my mind about going out. He was on his stomach in the entrance groaning, and I could see the wounds on his back and legs. I attempted to treat those superficial wounds, not knowing that he was badly wounded in the abdomen, and he died a few minutes later.

'I was now alone in the tent, hunkered down in the lava ash with my Colt 0.45-cal pointed at the door. I could hear the Japs running through the tent rows, talking and throwing grenades. Rifle rounds shredded the centre post of the tent.

'As daybreak approached, I could see light through dozens of small holes in the tent from grenade fragments. After it got good and light, I exited the tent and joined a young Marine a few yards away. He was throwing grenades over my tent, and Japanese grenades were coming back. We were hiding behind a stack of K rations by the mess tent. There was a Japanese bicycle lying in the ash a few feet in front of us. This Marine threw a grenade over my tent, and after the explosion a Jap hand came flying back over the tent and landed in the spokes of the bicycle. This is a very vivid memory of mine.'

Capt Felix Scott of the 46th FS was no stranger to sleeping in tents after having served with the squadron on Makin Island in 1943-44, but that did not prepare him for the events of 26 March;

'We were living in tents, four of us in each one. Explosions started going off all around. I thought we were being shelled from the sea. I figured they had their distance computed exactly on our tent, because explosives were hitting the tent, rolling off and exploding. There was a bomb crater about

Amongst the pilots to survive the tent attack on 26 March was Capt Felix Scott, who is seen here whilst still a first lieutenant during the Makin Island campaign. He shot down a Japanese night intruder in his P-39Q *TEXAS ED* during his 1943-44 combat tour. The experience of pilots such as Scott would be invaluable when 'The Sun Setters' began VLR operations over Japan (*Felix Scott*)

1Lt John F Galbraith of the 531st FS, seen here in the cockpit of a P-38 in Hawaii during 1944, won a citation for bravery as a result of his actions during the 26 March banzai raid against the 21st FG tent area. He went on to fly numerous missions over Japan in his unnamed P-51D 44-63934 (*John Galbraith*)

four feet from our tent, so I yelled for everyone to leave the tent and get in the crater. I then realised what was happening – the Japs were in bomb craters all around the pilots and throwing grenades on our tents, not doing much damage. You could hear all the Japs chattering, then a "Banzai", and one of them would charge the tent and cut it with a sword so they could throw grenades through the hole. That's when we would shoot at them with our Colt 0.45-cal pistols.

'Our dawn patrol flight were on their way to get airborne when the Japs attacked. When they heard the explosions, they returned to see what was going on. The pilots saw that the officers' tents were under attack, but that the Japanese weren't bothering with the airmen's tents across the road. They told us to run for the airmen's tents at the count of three, and we did. I ended up in a bomb crater with the S-2 officer, Capt Snyder.

'While we were waiting for the infantry to arrive, I heard a piece of shrapnel whistle through the air and hit Snyder on the leather jacket. He yelled, "They got me". I picked up the piece of hand grenade – about the size of a half dollar – and handed it to him. It hadn't penetrated his coat.

'Then, a captain and sergeant came in a Jeep with rifles and a flame thrower. They passed the rifles out and told us to follow them. The captain told the flame thrower to burn them out. They turned the flames on the bomb craters and burned all the tents that contained Japs. I think all the Japs were dead in an hour.'

Another pilot in the 46th FS, 1Lt John F Galbraith, received a citation for bravery exhibited on 26 March. He wrote a detailed account of his actions in a letter to his brother just a few days after the action;

'It was almost pitch dark outside when they charged into my tent, which was next to the road and near a Marine flame thrower dump. They ran down the rows of tents, pitching in hand grenades. I was in bed when the first one went off. Nearly a dozen exploded on and around our tent before I could get out of bed. Three of my buddies ran out into the area and jumped into fox holes – one came back about 0600 hrs when it was getting light.

'I took the responsibility of organising a defence of our tent, putting one fellow at the northwest corner with an M1 rifle, another on the east side with a Colt 0.45-cal pistol, and I took the south side and entrance myself – barricaded it with three sandbags, a B-4 bag, a five-gallon water can and a wash stand for additional cover and concealment. I was armed with a 0.30-cal carbine that I had only bought the night before from a Marine for one quart of whiskey!

'At about this time a Jap officer stopped at the northwest corner, where we had left a cover open, and started to throw in a grenade. I fired three shots through the tent in machine gun fashion, but Paul Schurr, a tent mate, dropped him with a 0.45-cal "slug". The Jap was dressed in a US field jacket and carried a carbine.

'Back to the front door, I laid down on the ground and rested my carbine on the sandbags. Soon the Japs started to cross the clearing between the tent rows. The range was roughly 10 yards, and since I could hit a dime at that distance I opened up on them. Within five minutes I had killed four of them – simply waited until they got midway between the tents and shot them through the body about five inches below the heart. When they fell, I shot them once more to make sure.

'Then I spotted two Jap officers running toward a tent two rows ahead of me. I motioned to the fellas in my tent, and we fired as they withdrew their swords. They wielded those swords with both hands and cut that tent like it was tissue paper. They never finished their job, though, for we opened fire with a hail of steel that would have killed a dozen of them. We then went back to our posts, and I killed four more that tried to cross the opening in the other direction.

'At this point they got wary and only one more tried to creep by. I shot him once, probably injuring him. As he crawled back out of view I shot

Propeller blades from a wrecked aircraft support the 21st FG sign at Central Field on Iwo Jima. 'Sun Setters' was the nickname chosen by VII Fighter Command to describe its mission (*Bob Sterritt*)

Maj Sam Hudson, popular 531st FS CO, never had the opportunity to lead his squadron on a VLR mission. On 26 March his left hand was badly mangled by an exploding grenade early in the banzai raid, and he was evacuated to the US for treatment. Hudson spent a year in various hospitals receiving treatment, including tendon grafts, before returning to flight status in 1946 (*John Galbraith*)

through the corner of the tent. I think I got him, but can't say definitely. Things quieted down for a while, except for a shower of hand grenades –they had only a few rifles, but bags of grenades.

'Then I got a bit of a scare. A giant Jap (six feet tall) walked around the tent directly next to me. He was looking around but failed to see me until it was too late. I shot him just as he turned to go into the tent, and he fell, but wasn't dead. He tried to get up on his elbows and I shot him twice more, the last time through his helmet just to make sure. About ten minutes later another walked up right behind his body and got the same dose. Maybe it sounds a bit gruesome, but it was easy to do. The screams of our guys that they hit alone were enough to give us the guts to do it, and besides, it was just what they were trying to do to me.

'About 0710 hrs, the Marines shouted to us left in the area to evacuate it and defend the enlisted men's area adjacent to ours. I told the fellas to follow me out at intervals, and I made a break for it, running at top speed, barefooted, with my carbine in my right hand and spare clips in my left.

'Just as I neared a big foxhole they hit me. My steel helmet saved my life, as a hand grenade exploded on the front rim of it, bending it all out of shape, cutting the rim off and splintering the liner. The blast was terrible, but luckily the shrapnel took only the skin off the left side of my nose, plus a few nicks here and there. The blast hemorrhaged my left eye and hurt my ears, but they are okay, and I can fly tomorrow. I managed to see through the blood well enough to make it to our lines, where I was led to an aid station and taken to a hospital for two-and-a-half days. The rest of my tent mates were okay, too, although two were hit with shrapnel while escaping the tent.'

Others were not so lucky as Galbraith and his tent mates. By the time the Marines arrived to mop up the remaining Japanese attackers, the 21st FG had suffered 14 men killed and 50 wounded. Among the more seriously wounded were 21st FG CO Col Ken Powell, who like Van Nada was sent to Hawaii to recover, and would return to lead his group over Japan, and Maj Sam Hudson, CO of the 531st FS. Hudson's left hand was badly mangled by an exploding grenade early in the raid, and he was evacuated to the US for treatment.

In a letter to Galbraith shortly before his death in 1993, Hudson recounted how he spent a year in various hospitals receiving treatment, including tendon grafts, before returning to flight status in 1946. He subsequently served as a meteorologist in the Air Weather Service before retiring from the military in 1961 and going on to a second career as a college professor.

The American 147th Infantry Regiment uses a bulldozer to bury Japanese soldiers in a mass grave on Iwo Jima after the 26 March banzai raid. An estimated 300 Japanese troops died in the night attack. This inscription was printed on the back of the photograph – 'Who mourns these poor souls who died in vain?' (*Ed Linfante*)

The banzai raid of 26 March proved the closing action of the ground campaign to take Iwo Jima, although small pockets of enemy troops remained to be rooted out by the American infantry on the island. In the 21st FG bivouac area, the men hastily abandoned their tents to dig foxholes, and the ground echelon arrived later in the day. Meanwhile, a company of the 147th Infantry Regiment was assigned to the airfield to provide perimeter guards.

The 21st FG, with Maj Elmer Booth temporarily replacing Col Powell as CO, immediately began flying strikes against the Bonin Islands. On 30 March the group suffered its first aerial fatality when 2Lt Albert J Tondora was killed in an aeroplane crash at Iwo.

But by this time all of 'Mickey' Moore's pilots on Iwo Jima were asking themselves the same question – When are we going to Tokyo? The answer was not long in coming.

This was the 4th Marine Division cemetery on Iwo Jima. The division paid a heavy price for its part in taking the island, its casualties numbering 9098 – almost half the division's strength. An estimated 22,000 Japanese were killed by the three Marine Corps divisions (3rd, 4th and 5th). Only 44 prisoners were taken by the 4th Division (*Ted Perritt*)

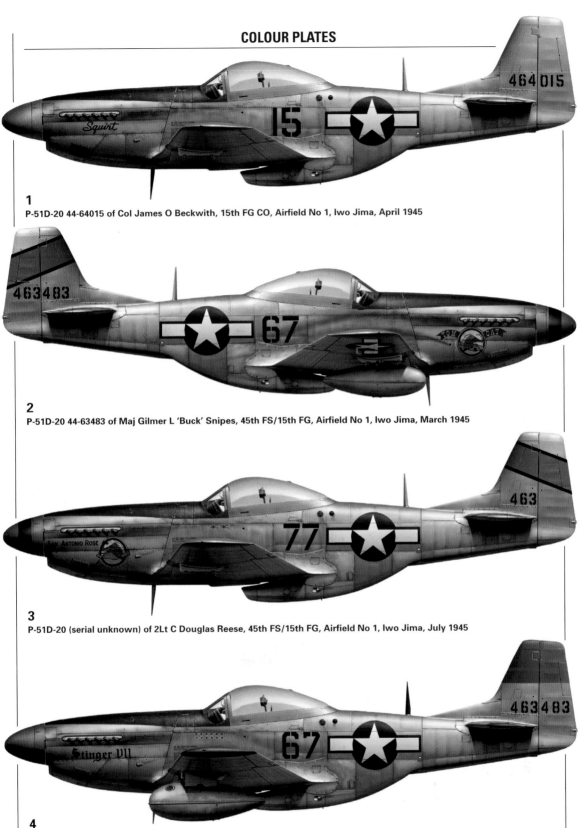

1
P-51D-20 44-64015 of Col James O Beckwith, 15th FG CO, Airfield No 1, Iwo Jima, April 1945

2
P-51D-20 44-63483 of Maj Gilmer L 'Buck' Snipes, 45th FS/15th FG, Airfield No 1, Iwo Jima, March 1945

3
P-51D-20 (serial unknown) of 2Lt C Douglas Reese, 45th FS/15th FG, Airfield No 1, Iwo Jima, July 1945

4
P-51D-20 44-63483 of Maj R W 'Todd' Moore, 45th FS/15th FG, Airfield No 1, Iwo Jima, August 1945

5
P-51D-20 44-63822 of Capt Walter H 'Sam' Powell, 47th FS/15th FG, Airfield No 1, Iwo Jima, April 1945

6
P-51D-20 44-63972 of 1Lt W Hayden Sparks, 47th FS/15th FG, Airfield No 1, Iwo Jima, May 1945

7
P-51D-20 44-63619 of 1Lt Harry M Tyler, 47th FS/15th FG, Airfield No 1, Iwo Jima, August 1945

8
P-51D-20 44-63973 of Maj James M Vande Hey, 78th FS/15th FG, Airfield No 1, Iwo Jima, April 1945

9
P-51D-20 44-63353 of 1Lt Doyle T Brooks Jr, 78th FS/15th FG, Airfield No 1, Iwo Jima, June 1945

10
P-51D-25 44-72641 of 2Lt Joseph P Gutierrez, 78th FS/15th FG, Airfield No 1, Iwo Jima, September 1945

11
P-51D-20 44-63755 of Maj Fred A Shirley, 46th FS/21st FG, Airfield No 2, Iwo Jima, April 1945

12
P-51D-20 44-63719 of 1Lt Victor F Kilkowski, 46th FS/21st FG, Airfield No 2, Iwo Jima, May 1945

13
P-51D-20 44-63898 of Capt Jack K Ort, 46th FS/21st FG, Airfield No 2, Iwo Jima, August 1945

14
P-51D-20 22-63451 of 1Lt Robert J Louwers, 46th FS/21st FG, Airfield No 2, Iwo Jima, June 1945

15
P-51D-20 44-63733 of Maj Paul W Imig, 72nd FS/21st FG, Airfield No 2, Iwo Jima, April 1945

16
P-51D-20 44-63756 of 1Lt Robert C Sterritt, 72nd FS/21st FG, Airfield No 2, Iwo Jima, August 1945

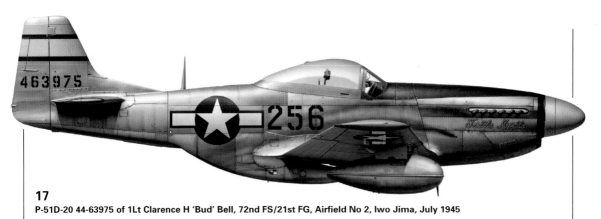

17
P-51D-20 44-63975 of 1Lt Clarence H 'Bud' Bell, 72nd FS/21st FG, Airfield No 2, Iwo Jima, July 1945

18
P-51D-25 44-73623 of Maj Harry C Crim Jr, 531st FS/21st FG, Airfield No 2, Iwo Jima, July 1945

19
P-51D-20 44-63781 of Capt Charles G Betz, 531st FS/21st FG, Airfield No 2, Iwo Jima, May 1945

20
P-51D-20 44-63934 of 1Lt John F Galbraith, 531st FS/21st FG, Airfield No 2, Iwo Jima, June 1945

21
P-51D-20 44-72557 of 1Lts John W Winnen and Philip G Alston, 457th FS/506th FG, Airfield No 3, I
wo Jima, summer 1945

22
P-51D-20 44-63291 of 1Lt Wesley A Murphey Jr, 457th FS/506th FG, Airfield No 3, Iwo Jima, Summer 1945

23
P-51D-25 44-72854 of Capts William B Lawrence Jr and Alan J Kinvig, 457th FS/506th FG, Airfield No 3,
Iwo Jima, summer 1945

24
P-51D-20 44-72607 of Maj Harrison E Shipman, 458th FS/506th FG, Airfield No 3, Iwo Jima, May 1945

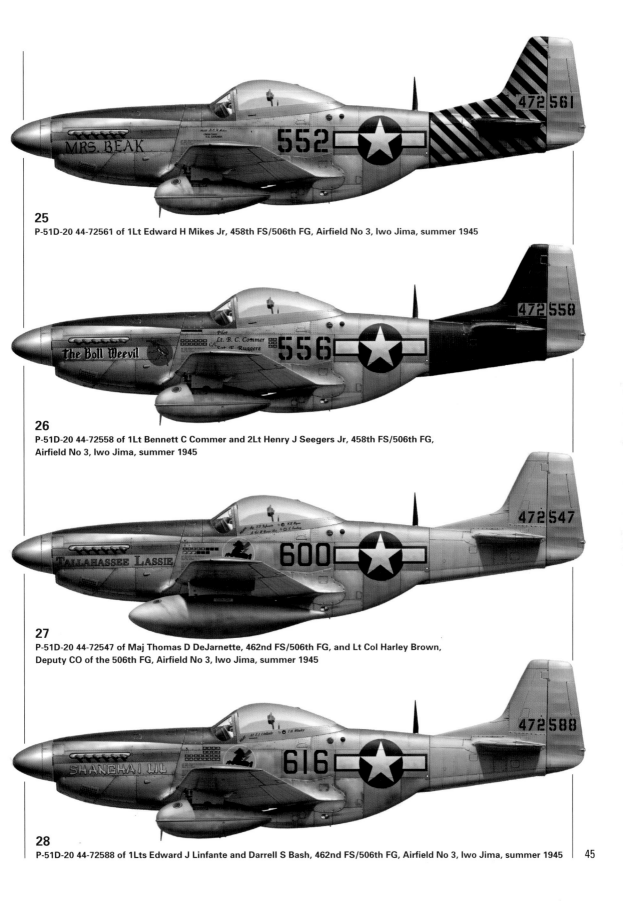

25
P-51D-20 44-72561 of 1Lt Edward H Mikes Jr, 458th FS/506th FG, Airfield No 3, Iwo Jima, summer 1945

26
P-51D-20 44-72558 of 1Lt Bennett C Commer and 2Lt Henry J Seegers Jr, 458th FS/506th FG, Airfield No 3, Iwo Jima, summer 1945

27
P-51D-20 44-72547 of Maj Thomas D DeJarnette, 462nd FS/506th FG, and Lt Col Harley Brown, Deputy CO of the 506th FG, Airfield No 3, Iwo Jima, summer 1945

28
P-51D-20 44-72588 of 1Lts Edward J Linfante and Darrell S Bash, 462nd FS/506th FG, Airfield No 3, Iwo Jima, summer 1945

29
P-51D-20 44-72587 of 2Lts James R Bercaw and William G Ebersole, 462nd FS/506th FG, Airfield No 3,
Iwo Jima, summer 1945

30
P-51D-25 44-72855 of 1Lts Allen F Colley and Leonard A Dietz, 462nd FS/506th FG, Airfield No 3, Iwo Jima, summer 1945

Profile 14 artwork close-up

LITTLE FRIENDS OVER JAPAN

By late March 1945 XXI Bomber Command's B-29s had been fire-bombing Tokyo at night for several months, laying waste to vast sections of the city. But key industrial targets remained that could only be hit by precision daylight bombing. Experience had shown that bombing accuracy suffered on high-altitude raids, but if the B-29s came in at lower levels they became vulnerable to enemy flak and fighter interception. Gen LeMay needed 'Mickey' Moore's Mustangs to provide escort for his Superfortresses, and the 'Sun Setters' were eager to start providing it.

So as the last stench of battle from the Japanese banzai raid cleared from the air on Iwo Jima, nearly 100 P-51s of the 15th and 21st FGs fired up at their airfields on 30 March for their first long-range mission. However, the aeroplanes would not be flying north to Japan, and possible air combat, on this day. Instead, they would be heading south to Saipan and back on a final practice mission, before being turned loose against the enemy. The results of this flight might have given LeMay cause for concern, as less than half of the Mustangs completed it successfully. The rest fell victim to a variety of problems, some returning to Iwo early and others landing at Saipan for repairs.

At VII Fighter Command headquarters, the staff went to work studying the navigational problems, fuel consumption, weather, pilot fatigue,

Pilots were briefed prior to each mission in this Quonset hut and then de-briefed by their squadron intelligence officers in the same building when they returned. After 7+ hours in the cockpit of a P-51, most pilots were too tired and sore to have much enthusiasm for post-mission interviews (*Bob Louwers*)

Filling in for the injured Col Ken Powell, Maj DeWitt Spain (right) led the 21st FG on the group's first mission to Tokyo on 7 April. Seen here after the operation, Spain is talking with Brig Gen 'Mickey' Moore (centre) and Maj Harry Crim, 531st FS CO and future ace. Crim scored the first two of his eventual six victories that day. The 531st FS Mustang behind them is *"VEE'S MALE"*, squadron number and serial unknown (*Tom Ivie*)

mechanical failures and other weaknesses revealed by the practice mission. Within a few days they had sorted out most of the issues, and were ready to commit the P-51s to battle.

Bad weather intruded during the first few days of April, but finally on the 6th everything was in readiness to send the Mustangs to Tokyo for the first time the following day. The mission given to VII Fighter Command tasked it with providing 108 P-51s from the 15th and 21st FG as escorts for 107 B-29s of the 73rd BW that were heading for Target 357 – Nakajima aircraft engine factories on the west side of the city.

All six squadrons from the two Mustang groups were to take part, and it was a measure of the experience level in VII Fighter Command that only pilots with more than 600 hours in fighters were chosen to fly this important first mission.

Mission leader Col Beckwith led four flights from the 47th FS aloft from South Field at 0655 hrs on 7 April 1945, thus kicking off VII Fighter Command's historic first Empire mission. Maj DeWitt Spain, leading the 21st FG in place of the convalescing Col Ken Powell, took off from Central Field with his three squadrons at about the same time.

Following Beckwith as leader of the 47th's 'Green Flight' was a familiar face – Brig Gen 'Mickey' Moore. The groups formed up on Beckwith as he led them north to Kita Rock, where they would rendezvous with three navigating B-29s. Beckwith got no farther than that, as the oxygen system in his Mustang (44-64015) failed and he broke off to return to base. That left 47th FS CO Maj John Piper as mission leader.

Soon, Brig Gen Moore discovered that the switch controlling the fuel tanks in his fighter was stuck, so he too was forced to head back to Iwo Jima. Two more disappointed senior officers would have been hard to find in the entire Pacific Theatre that day.

In all, 17 Mustangs aborted the mission after take-off, and the rest settled down for the three-hour flight to Japan at 10,000 ft. Fuel management was critical. The Mustang was equipped with internal fuel tanks in both wings, plus one behind the pilot's seat and a 110-gallon drop tank hung from each wing.

Normally possessed of good manoeuvrability, the P-51 became something of a tail-heavy slouch when the fuselage tank was full, so it was imperative to burn off most of its fuel before encountering enemy aircraft in the target area. Likewise, the drop tanks would be jettisoned prior to a combat engagement, so it was also prudent to burn off as much of the fuel in them as possible before that happened, leaving the internal fuel supply for combat and the return trip to Iwo Jima.

Groundcrewmen gather in front of 45th FS Mustangs on the flightline at South Field while preparing the fighters for a mission. Closest to the camera is *San Antonio Rose*, which was assigned to 1Lt Doug Reese after his first P-51 was wrecked by another pilot (*Tom Ivie*)

P-51D 44-63420 heads this line-up of 47th FS aircraft on Iwo Jima. Later nicknamed *Moonbeam McSwine* in the normal fashion of the 47th FS 'Dogpatchers', this aircraft flew many Empire missions before it was damaged in a landing accident by 1Lt Martin Gilbride on 9 August 1945. Iwo Jima-based P-51s, such as these from the 47th FS, carried two 110-gallon drop tanks on escort missions to give them sufficient range to fly to Japan and back. Normal procedure was to drop the tanks when making landfall on the Japanese coast (*Steve Moseley*)

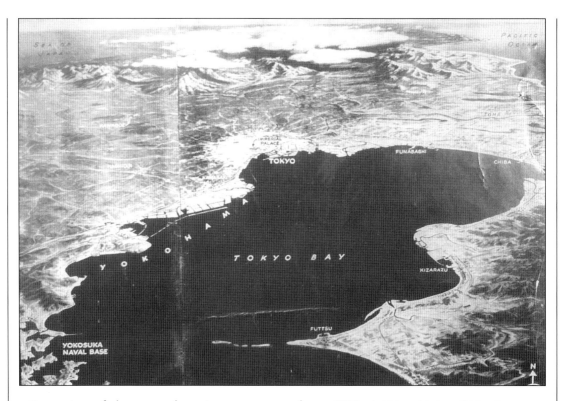

For maximum fuel economy, the engines were set to run lean at 1750-1900 rpm, with manifold pressure of 34 to 35 inches. One pilot recalled that the propeller turned so slowly at this setting that he could almost see its four blades as they turned in front of him.

The Mustangs rendezvoused with the B-29s over Kozu Rock, just off the coast of Japan, at 1020 hrs. The bombers were at 15,000 ft, and the P-51s fanned out into combat formation several thousand feet above them, with the 21st FG on the left and the 15th FG on the right. The formation hit landfall within ten minutes, and soon enemy interceptors were spotted over Sagami Wan (Tokyo Bay) between Atami and Hiratsuka, 30 to 45 miles south of the target. The Mustang pilots quickly jettisoned their drop tanks and went to full power, gunsights switched on.

'Blue Flight' of the 46th FS/21st FG had the first crack at them when several pilots got hits on a Ki-44 Shoki in the vicinity of Yokohama. Before long, the Mustangs were scrapping with single- and twin-engined Japanese fighters all over the sky.

The 47th FS/15th FG made first contact at 1040 hrs, when Maj Piper's 'Red Flight' spotted a Ki-45 Toryu about 900 ft above them, flying a parallel course. The P-51 pilots gave chase until the twin-engined fighter did a split-S and dove away, then they resumed their escort position.

Next, they spotted four dark green Ki-44 Shokis approaching head-on, but these fighters also broke away into a dive when the Mustangs approached. The flight was still over the bay, just off Tokyo, when the engine in Maj Piper's P-51 abruptly quit. He turned back out to sea with his wingman, 1Lt Joe Brunette, and by the time Piper's engine restarted the formation was long gone. The pair proceeded to the Rally Point,

This aerial view of Tokyo Bay, as seen from the south, became very familiar to the pilots of VII Fighter Command after their initial VLR mission on 7 April 1945. With the completion of just one flight to the city, pilots were considered members of the 'Tokyo Club'. Some went so far as to decorate the backs of their flight jackets with the 'club's' logo (*John Galbraith*)

picked up a heading for Iwo Jima and settled down in their cockpits for the long flight home.

Capt Sam Powell and 1Lt Frank Ayres formed the second element of 'Red Flight', and they also broke off early when the latter reported his fuel supply was running low. When 200 miles from Iwo Jima, Ayres was nearly out of fuel. Spotting the rescue destroyer USS *Cassin* at the 'Warcloud' rendezvous point, he bailed out and was quickly picked up unharmed.

The 47th FS's 'Yellow Flight', led by Capt Ray Obenshain, also had no opportunity to close with the enemy. The flight held its position as various enemy fighters made feints at the B-29s before breaking away. They noted heavy flak over the target and saw two B-29s blown out of the sky, with no parachutes spotted, before turning for home.

Capt Bob Down had assumed the lead of the 47th FS's 'Green Flight' after Brig Gen Moore, followed by Maj Emmett Kearney, aborted the mission. While still over Sagami Bay at 18,000 ft, Down and his element leader, 1Lt Dick Hintermeier, spotted a Ki-45 approaching from the northeast.

Hintermeier, a combat veteran who had scored a victory with the 45th FS during the Marshall Islands campaign, turned into the Toryu for a high frontal pass and put a burst into its right engine, which began to smoke. Then Down whipped in behind the smoking fighter and fired two bursts. The first hit the Toryu's canopy, and the second blasted the right engine again, causing the stricken fighter to fall away in flames. Down and Hintermeier were given shared credit for the Ki-45, which was deemed to be the first enemy aircraft shot down by USAAF fighters over Japan.

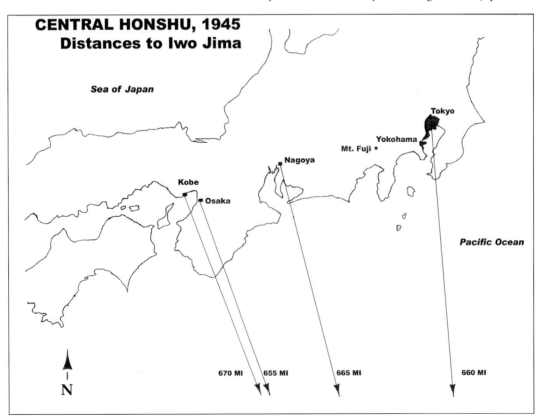

Capt Down shot down a Ki-44 a few moments later. Then his wingman, 1Lt Eurich Bright, got into the act by attacking a Ki-61 Hein from the rear and setting it on fire. Bright overran the inline-engine fighter, which was beginning to break apart, so he pulled up and saw it fall in flames. About then an A6M Zero made a pass at Bright, who manoeuvred out of the line of fire and latched onto the Zero's tail as it dove away. With Capt Down keeping Bright's tail clear, the latter fired from dead astern. The Zero pulled up, burning, and then fell off in a final death dive.

Bright was not finished, however, as he then spotted a twin-engined aircraft and shot it down from behind for his third victory of the mission. Bright's last target was another Zero, but he lost it in a split-S, so 'Green Flight' turned south for an uneventful flight home.

Capt Ed Markham was leading 'Blue Flight' of the 47th at 17,000 ft out ahead of the B-29s, about 20 miles south of the target, when he encountered a single-engined two-seater that he identified as a Nakajima C6N 'Myrt' JNAF reconnaissance aircraft. 'Blue Flight' approached it from behind, bracketing the aeroplane, which then turned into the second element, led by 1Lt Richard Condrick. He fired two bursts and hit the 'Myrt' in the left wing root, setting it on fire. The C6N went down trailing smoke, and it was seen to crash into the ground. At this point, the two elements became separated.

As Markham approached Tokyo, he spotted two Ki-45s about 1000 ft below him, heading in the same direction. He closed in to about 250 ft behind one of them and gave it a long burst. The aeroplane broke up in the air and fell away as Markham and his wingman watched. The 'Blue Flight' elements made several more passes at enemy fighters but did not score

A groundcrewman turns to watch as a P-51 comes in to land at South Field. In the foreground is the nose of *Shadrach* of the 45th FS. Note the squadron badge painted on the cowling. This aeroplane was assigned to 1Lt Doug Reese when the squadron first arrived on Iwo Jima (*Tom Ivie*)

These were the pilots who made the 47th FS the top-scoring 'Sun Setter' squadron on 7 April 1945, with seven confirmed victories and two aircraft damaged. They are, from left to right, 1Lt Dick Hintermeier, Capt Ed Markham, 1Lt Eurich Bright, Capt Bob Down and 1Lt Richard 'Spider' Condrick. No P-51s were lost during the mission. The 47th FS maintained the scoring lead throughout the VLR campaign, tallying 40 confirmed aerial victories by VJ-Day (*Tom Ivie*)

again before turning south toward the Rally Point, where they joined up with B-29s for the three-hour flight back to Iwo Jima.

The 45th FS was led by its CO, Maj Buck Snipes. Like Maj Piper, he had trouble with his fuel tanks and lost power briefly just as the squadron began to encounter enemy aircraft. Snipes' P-51 lost several thousand feet before the pilot succeeded in restarting its engine, and he then climbed back up into position at the head of 'Red Flight'. Soon, he spotted a Ki-61 1000 ft above him, and so pulled his nose up for a shot. Snipes could not get proper deflection to hit the aeroplane, but his wingman, 1Lt Herb Henderson, put a few 'slugs' into it before the Japanese pilot made his escape.

The Mustangs reformed, and soon Snipes put a burst from behind into a Ki-44, which began to smoke from the trailing edge of its wing before Snipes overran his target and lost it. Henderson, meanwhile, had attacked the Ki-44's wingman. The Shoki turned left, which put it right in front of Snipes, who promptly opened fire. The burst from the Mustang's six 0.50-cal guns tore the Nakajima fighter apart, and the stricken machine dropped for several thousand feet before Snipes and Henderson saw the pilot bail out.

As this was going on, the second element of 'Red Flight' attacked a Ki-61 that was attempting to make a pass at the B-29s. Capt Al Maltby, element leader, pulled straight up and put a good burst into the Hein before stalling out. His wingman, 1Lt Wes Brown, followed the stricken enemy fighter long enough to observe it dropping out of control straight down, unlikely to recover.

The pair reformed and headed for Tokyo, where they saw a twin-engined Japanese aeroplane drop a phosphorus bomb on the B-29 formation. They latched onto the fighter, believed to be a Ki-45, and Brown sent it falling away in a tight spiral to its destruction.

Capt Art Bridge, leading 'Blue Flight' of the 45th FS, lost contact with 'Red Flight' after making landfall. All four members of this flight were highly experienced veterans of the Marshalls campaign, and it soon began to show. As the flight neared Tokyo, Capt George Hunter took a snap shot at a passing Ki-45 from his 'Blue 4' position and was rewarded by seeing a sparkle of hits as the aeroplane passed from view.

Just west of Hiratsuka, a flight of four Ki-44s attacked 'Blue Flight' at 18,000 ft. 'Blue 3', Capt Bruce Campbell, and Hunter turned into the attack and concentrated their fire on the same Shoki, which went down in flames. Bridge and his wingman, 1Lt George Dunlap, also attacked, and the former saw his tracers rip into one of the Ki-44s at its wing root before the aeroplane made a split-S and disappeared. Bridge became separated from the rest of 'Blue Flight' during this encounter, but all four Mustangs returned home safely.

'Green Flight' of the 45th FS flew all the way to the target area without engaging enemy fighters. The flight was at 17,000 ft when Capt Mort Knox, element leader, spotted a JNAF N1K Shiden fighter flying parallel to the bombers down and to his right. He dove behind the naval fighter and gave it one good burst from dead astern, which tore up its tail and set the aeroplane on fire. The remaining three pilots in the flight also attacked the Shiden as it began to fall out of control, but Knox was given credit for the victory.

'Green 2', 1Lt Joe Walker, also got hits from 60 degrees deflection on a Ki-45 that was attacking the B-29s, but the aeroplane was able to complete its pass and dive away.

'Yellow Flight' leader Capt Walt Morey lost his wingman near the target when 1Lt Quentin McCorkle accidentally hit the mixture switch and killed his engine. McCorkle's aeroplane dropped 8000 ft before he managed to restart the engine. As he climbed back toward his flight,

The original markings of the 78th FS Mustangs are visible in this flightline view. Nearest to the camera is *Nina Lou II* (44-63407), whose regular pilot was 1Lt Arden Gibson. The third aircraft in line is *Dee Bee II*, flown by 1Lt Douglas B 'DB' Moore (*Tom Ivie*)

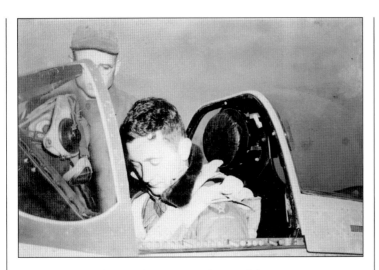

McCorkle crossed over the B-29s, and one of the American gunners opened fire on him. The P-51 took two hits but did not sustain serious damage. Otherwise, 'Yellow Flight's' mission was uneventful.

All aeroplanes from the 45th FS were back on the ground at Iwo Jima by 1745 hrs.

The 78th FS, led by CO Maj Jim Vande Hey, was positioned at the right front quarter of the formation, and thus was able to claim the honour of being the first USAAF fighter squadron to fly over Tokyo. 1Lt Charles Heil claimed another distinction for the 78th by mistake. Losing contact with his flight at the outbound rendezvous, Heil latched onto the first formation of B-29s he saw and stayed with them all the way to their target and back. He did not find out until later that these B-29s were on a separate mission to bomb Nagoya without escort. By going with them, Heil became the first USAAF fighter pilot to fly over Nagoya, and the only pilot to escort an entire formation of B-29s by himself!

Maj Vande Hey, leading 'Red Flight', was over Kiratsuka when he heard the bombers call in a bogey attacking from '12 o'clock high'. With 'Yellow Flight' providing top cover, he quickly spotted a Ki-45 making the pass, and damaged it with a deflection shot. The major described the twin-engined aeroplane as black, with orange zebra stripes on the wings and fuselage. He had better results a few moments later when he attacked a Ki-46 as it was making a shallow diving turn to the right.

'I closed rapidly, firing long bursts, and saw my hits strike the left engine and the wing root, causing debris to fly off the aeroplane', he reported. 'The left engine then suddenly flamed and I had to break off'. The 'Yellow Flight' leader, Capt Vic Mollan, observed the Ki-46 falling in a steep spiral, trailing smoke, and Vande Hey was credited with a victory.

The leader of 'Blue Flight' was Maj Jim Tapp, the 78th FS operations officer. Shortly after making landfall on the west side of Tokyo Bay, Tapp spotted a Ki-45 diving on the B-29s and gave chase. He closed in on the Toryu and opened fire at a range of 300 yards, putting a long burst into the fighter's right engine, and also getting incendiary strikes on the fuselage. Tapp's wingman, 1Lt Phil Maher, fired at the Ki-45 too, but the Toryu did not catch fire or appear to go out of control as 'Blue Flight' broke off contact and climbed back to position over the bombers at 20,000 ft.

Tapp next spotted a Ki-61 Hein about three miles ahead and gave chase. He cut back the throttle as he approached from behind so as not to overrun and fired at the Hein from 800 ft down to about 100 ft. The fighter soon caught fire, and the pilot was seen to bail out for Tapp's first victory of the day.

He was far from finished, as the Mustang pilot next attacked a Ki-46 that was making a head-on pass against the bombers, but was unable to observe results. 'Blue Flight' then dropped back to give support to a burning B-29 that was under attack from a silver two-seat enemy aircraft of unidentified type. Tapp began his pass at 90 degrees deflection, opened fire at 1000 ft and closed up right behind his target. He saw pieces of the aircraft breaking off and strikes all over the fuselage, before it flipped over into a spin. 1Lt Maher watched as the stricken aeroplane crashed into the ground.

'Blue Flight' moved back into its escort position, and then spotted six single-engined enemy fighters – four A6Ms and two Ki-44s – approaching at 18,000 ft. Tapp made a head-on pass at one of the Shokis and saw his fire hitting the engine and cockpit. The aeroplane went into a violent spin as Tapp passed, and 1Lt Maher saw a six-foot section of wing break off as it fell from the sky, disintegrating as it went. When the mission reports were turned in, VII Fighter Command gave Tapp a victory credit for the first Ki-45 he attacked, plus the three single-engine victims, making him top scorer for the day with four confirmed victories.

'Green Flight' of the 78th FS was led by Capt R H 'Todd' Moore, another veteran of the Marshall Islands campaign with one kill in P-40s to his credit. The flight didn't engage the enemy until reaching the Choshi area, where Moore spotted four A6M3 'Hamp' naval fighters doing 'lazy eights' in string formation over the B-29s at 22,000 ft.

Moore latched onto the end of the string and opened fire on the aeroplane in front of him from 20 degrees deflection, causing it to explode. At full throttle, he next closed in on the number three fighter in the string at the bottom of the 'lazy eight' and hit it in the engine and cockpit with a short burst that set it on fire.

Capt Ernie Hostetler, 'Blue Flight' element leader, then called Moore to warn him that the lead 'Hamp' was about to attack, so Moore broke off into a dive. His wingman, 1Lt Robert Roseberry, noted that the entire bottom of the enemy aeroplane his leader had just attacked was blown out and burning as it fell from the sky for Moore's second victory of the day.

All Mustangs of the 78th FS returned safely to Iwo Jima, the last landing at 1415 hrs.

The 21st FG, in its position on the left side of the bomber formation, saw far less action than the 15th FG on 7 April because the Japanese interceptions came primarily from the east. Leading the 531st FS was its new CO, Capt Harry C Crim Jr, the ex-72nd FS operations officer having assumed command of the 531st after Maj Hudson was wounded in the banzai raid. Crim had flown a combat tour on P-38 Lightnings with the 14th FG in the MTO during 1943 without scoring a victory and was eager to make his mark, as would soon become obvious.

Nine of the 20 P-51s in the 531st FS aborted the mission, leaving Crim with a short squadron to perform its share of the escort duties. His 'Red Flight' was first into the target area, and soon spotted about 30 enemy fighters of various types, all apparently operating independently of each other. Crim made the following report of the ensuing action;

'My flight was over a bomber box just south of Tokyo when a "Zeke" was reported at "six o'clock high". My flight turned 180 degrees and the "Zeke" passed overhead. At this time I saw a "Tony" going in the opposite direction about 1000 ft lower. I made an overhead attack on him but couldn't get the right amount of lead, so on the recovery from 500 ft below I gave him a short burst from close range. Overshooting, I pulled up over him and rolled on my back. From this position, I could see the left side of his engine burning. He then started about a one-needle-width turn to the left, and I dropped back on his tail. From this position I fired a three- or four-second burst from about 300 ft. His right wing came off at the middle panel.

'I broke off to the right and saw a "Nick" at about two miles at "three o'clock" to me, same level, making a large circle to the left. I cut his circle and started firing at about 700 ft at 30 degrees, and I fired until I overshot. I pulled up on the outside of his turn and then dropped back on his tail. His left engine nacelle and left wing were burning as I closed in on the second attack. I fired again until I overran, at which time his fuselage was starting to burn. I pulled up and circled once and headed for the Rally Point. I was looking back constantly, and saw him crash into the southeastern suburbs of Tokyo.'

More than two years after flying his first combat mission, the aggressive pilot from Florida was finally on the scoreboard.

The element leader of 'Red Flight', 1Lt Robert G Anderson, was not so fortunate. Losing Capt Crim, Anderson led his wingman, 1Lt Lloyd Bosley, eastward across Tokyo Bay. Bosley reported;

'I was flying with my element leader at 12,000 ft when slightly to the right and below about 500 ft I saw a silver aeroplane. It passed under us to the left and I recognised it as a "Tony". My element leader dived on him, and as he made a sharp turn to the right my element leader gave a short burst with no effects. I turned with the "Tony" and started firing with a two radii lead. Not seeing any hits I began increasing my lead. With about $2^1/_2$ to $2^3/_4$ radii lead, I observed incendiaries bursting at and around his wing roots. Pieces of the aeroplane began pulling off. I kept firing for about 120 degrees turn, then the aeroplane turned over on its back and started spinning. I broke off and watched it spin down to about 5000 ft. Then I pulled up and rejoined my element leader.'

Shortly after the engagement, Bosley observed 1Lt Anderson do a roll-and-a-half over onto his back as if entering a split-S dive. Instead, Anderson's P-51 shed its wings and

With drop tanks still in place, a 72nd FS P-51 cavorts in the clouds. On 7 April 1945, the squadron claimed its first kills over Tokyo when Capt Adolph Bregar downed a Ki-45, 1Lt Jacob Gotwals got a Ki-44 and 1Lt William Merritt destroyed a Ki-44 and a Ki-61 (*Bob Sterritt*)

72nd FS pilot 1Lt Jacob W Gotwals Jr, who scored one victory on 7 April 1945, poses with his shot up P-51D 44-63981 after the mission of 11 June. The fighter returned to service on 22 July. By war's end 44-63981 had completed 19 missions following aborts on 16 and 19 April (*Bob Sterritt*)

exploded for no apparent reason. The three remaining 'Red Flight' Mustangs turned for home individually, but the other two 531st FS flights, which had not engaged the enemy, returned to Iwo intact. 1Lt Anderson was the only pilot of VII Fighter Command to be killed on the mission.

The 72nd FS, meanwhile, got four victories during the scrap. The squadron was the last to engage, with 1Lts Jacob W Gotwals Jr and William E Merritt each claiming a Ki-44 Shoki destroyed over Tokyo in engagements that began at 1055 hrs. A few minutes later, Capt Adolph J Bregar claimed a Ki-45 shot down, and Merritt scored again when he destroyed a Ki-61 while leaving the Tokyo area.

When the 'Sun Setters' tallied the results of the mission, 'Mickey' Moore had reason to be pleased, despite his personal disappointment at missing the action. The Mustang pilots were credited with 26 Japanese aeroplanes destroyed, one probably destroyed and five damaged, at a cost of two P-51s and one pilot. Only three Superfortresses went down during the mission – two hit by flak and one struck by an aerial bomb dropped on the formation.

If Gen LeMay had been concerned before the mission about the ability of Moore's P-51s to protect his B-29s, he could quit worrying now. The 'Little Friends', as the B-29s crews called the escorts, could do the job.

LESSONS LEARNED

The men of VII Fighter Command had reason to feel proud, and maybe even a little cocky, after their success of 7 April. But in war, a man's focus is on today and maybe tomorrow, not yesterday. In reality, 7 April was just the opening bell of Round One. There was a whole lot more fighting ahead in this bout.

The second VLR mission, on 12 April 1945, promised to be a near copy of the first, as the Mustangs again would escort B-29s of the 73rd BW attacking the Nakajima aircraft engine factories. The only difference in the plan was that the mission would kick off an hour later, with the Mustangs beginning their take-off rolls at 0800 hrs. On this day, however, VII Fighter Command would learn that missions do not always go as planned.

Right off the bat there was trouble at Central Airfield, where the 21st FG Mustangs encountered windy conditions while taxiing out. Some had to switch runways before taking off, which cost them precious time and fuel. Maj Elmer E Booth, deputy 21st FG commander and group leader, got off on time at 0755 hrs with the 46th FS, but the last aeroplane of his third squadron (the 531st FS) did not bring up the rear until 0837 hrs. By now, the 46th and 72nd FS were long gone, and eventually all three flights of the 531st returned to base without reaching Japan.

By the time the Mustangs reached Japan, various problems had reduced their number to just 82. They did their best to rendezvous with the B-29s, but the bomber formation was strung out and unwieldy. To add to that, the sky was hazy over Japan, with visibility down to four to eight miles.

The two remaining squadrons of the 21st FG took the high lead position for this mission, and at 1130 hrs the 46th FS began to encounter enemy interceptors.

46th FS commander Maj Fred Shirley made the initial contact. A combat veteran with 19 missions in the 45th FS during the Marshall Islands campaign, Shirley spotted a Ki-45 Toryu below him attempting to attack the B-29s and shot it down in a diving pass. Reforming his flight, Shirley next spotted a V-formation of JNAF J2M Raiden fighters and again swooped to attack. This time, kills went to Maj Shirley and 1Lts

Capt Walter H 'Sam' Powell of the 47th FS was taking off for the 12 April mission when he got caught in a crosswind and ground-looped *Li'l Butch* (44-63822). He missed another good day for his squadron, which came back to Iwo Jima with six more victories to its credit (*Tom Ivie*)

59

Trouble on the way – a flight of four 45th FS P-51s heads north toward Tokyo. They are, from left to right, *Victory Belle* (44-63325), 44-63314, *Foxy* (44-63474) and 44-63428. Two of these aeroplanes (44-63314 and 44-63474) were later written off in accidents on Iwo Jima (*Tom Ivie*)

John W Brock and Eugene V Naber, with Capt Jack V Garnett claiming a probable.

The 72nd FS, meanwhile, failed to close with the interceptors. But on the return flight to the Rally Point one flight was attacked by a particularly aggressive J2M pilot, and 1Lt James H Beattie was shot down and killed.

The 15th FG was led by Maj Emmett L 'Pilot Ben' Kearney Jr, deputy group commander, at the head of 'Red Flight' in the 47th FS. One of the

Looking very pleased with themselves after the second Empire mission, on 12 April, are Capt Lyman F Ennis of the 45th FS (left) and his wingman, 1Lt Alvan E Roberts Jr, who shared a Ki-45 destroyed. Behind them is the P-51 assigned to Capt Ennis, *MISS CORDIE* (*Tom Ivie*)

old 'Pineapple' pilots of VII Fighter Command, Kearney was about to get his first, and only, crack at air-to-air combat.

'Red Flight' made landfall at 1150 hrs and weaved over the bombers until just beyond the turning point, when the Mustang pilots spotted a lone Ki-45 passing below them, headed in the opposite direction. Maj Kearney and his wingman, 1Lt Harry M Tyler, performed a split-S onto the twin-engined fighter's tail and opened fire. The Toryu was hit, and they saw it fall off in a dive for 10,000 ft trailing smoke. The Mustangs pulled back up and reformed with 1Lt Alex Trodahl, who had been flying solo as the second element since his leader aborted earlier in the mission.

At this point, they spotted two more Ki-45s behind and below them. Kearney led the Mustangs in a 180-degree turn that brought them out on the tail of the left Ki-45, which he and Tyler both shot up. The left engine caught on fire, and the stricken aeroplane went straight down trailing a plume of smoke. Trodahl was able to see it crash into the ground after he had fired at another Ki-45 on the right, which was out of range. 'Red Flight' had one more encounter, when Kearney shot down an A6M Zero, before turning for home.

In all, the 15th FG tallied 11 confirmed victories, five probables and two damaged for the mission. Of these, the 78th FS contributed just one victory and one probable, but the victory was historic.

Maj Jim Tapp, leading his flight at the extreme right flank of the formation, spotted a Ki-61 Hein below him and shot it down in a diving

2Lt John W Brock (left) of the 46th FS notched up his first confirmed victory (a J2M Raiden) on 12 April. Shown here later in the campaign after he had become a flight commander, Brock scored a total of three victories flying P-51 *Slow Roll* (44-63891). Next to him, from left, are 1Lts Bob Louwers, Otis Erwin and Robert Campbell (*Bob Louwers*)

pass. Unfortunately, Tapp's wingman, 1Lt Fred W White, was following him so closely that the spent shells from Tapp's guns apparently got sucked into his Mustang's air scoop and damaged the radiator. White's engine failed on the flight home and he attempted to bail out, but his parachute did not open and he fell to his death. The 78th FS also lost 1Lt Gordon A Christoe, who went down over Japan during the fight.

At the time, this was thought to be Tapp's fourth victory, because he had turned in one of the four claims on 7 April as a probable. Some weeks later, VII Fighter Command reviewed his claims and upgraded the probable to a confirmed victory, making Tapp's 12 April kill his fifth. This was a minor point, because Tapp would score again on 19 April to be recognised as the first ace on Iwo Jima anyway.

When he filed his report on the mission, Maj Kearney complimented 1Lt Trodahl for staying with him as a one-aeroplane second element, and maintaining a perfect supporting position throughout the mission. Sadly, Trodahl would be killed later in the month when his engine failed on take-off for a mission.

Kearney also complained of continuing problems with gun stoppages on the P-51s in his report, stating that his own aeroplane was down to four functioning guns during the fight, and Trodahl had only two guns firing. This was perhaps attributable to the fine-grain volcanic dust on Iwo Jima, considering the P-51D had been operating in the European Theatre for nearly a year with minimal gun failures.

But the bigger problem was in the mission planning and execution. When the air fighting subsided, the Mustang pilots turned south for the long flight back to Iwo Jima. The problems at the start of the mission, and their 'round-about' escort route now started to hound them, because many of the Mustangs had been operating on internal fuel at high throttle settings for nearly an hour during the combat engagement.

The volcanic dust on Iwo Jima wreaked havoc on the engines of the 'Sun Setters' P-51s, with the 531st FS losing two Mustangs in the same week during April when their motors quit on take-off, forcing the pilots to belly-land them. *JEANETTE* was wrecked by either 1Lt Dale F Meyer on 16 April or by 1Lt William N Steele on 21 April (*Tom Ivie*)

The pilot, likely 1Lt Leo Evans, unbuckles from 78th FS P-51D *Wee Lona Lee* (44-63391) after a mission with help from his groundcrew. He has parked next to one of the B-29 navigator aeroplanes that led VII Fighter Command P-51s to and from Japan on their VLR missions (*Charles Butler*)

Desperate to get home, pilots began filling the radio channels with requests to the navigator B-29s for direct vectors to Iwo, or for directions to the nearest air-sea rescue units stationed along the route. In the event, only one more pilot went down on his way home – 1Lt Maurice F Gourley of the 47th FS – but many others were flying on fumes when they landed at Iwo Jima that day. Maj Jim Vande Hey, 78th FS CO, felt his engine quit just as he touched down on the runway at Airfield No 1. He was out of gas, and had to be towed in to his parking place. Like many other pilots, he had been in the air for a little over eight hours.

The next Empire mission was scheduled for 16 April, but the problems uncovered on the 12th were too complex to be sorted out in just four days. To make matters worse, the mission was changed at the last minute from another Tokyo escort to a sweep of enemy airfields in southern Kyushu, where kamikaze attacks were being launched against the American invasion fleet off Okinawa. The 15th FG was assigned as the low-level assault unit, with the 21st FG providing top cover. The mission produced eight more hours of trauma for the Mustang pilots, and little else.

The 21st FG was late getting off, causing the rendezvous to be delayed, and then had no fewer than 17 aircraft abort the mission. Two 21st FG pilots experienced mechanical failures that forced them to bail out en route to Kyushu, and one of them, 1Lt Glenn Reagan of the 72nd FS, was killed. Reaching Japan, the formation encountered no enemy interceptors over the target area.

Only two of the 15th FG squadrons were able to find a target, Kanoya Airfield, and it was relatively bare of aircraft. The Mustang attack produced few results, but several P-51s were hit by ground fire and had to limp home. One more pilot, 1Lt James R Wightman of the 78th FS, experienced engine failure on the return flight and bailed out, only to be killed when his parachute failed to open.

In mid-April, the USAAF's complex scheme for rotating pilots home based on points accrued during service in a combat zone began to take effect in VII Fighter Command, and it started near the top. Among the pilots to receive orders reassigning them to stateside duty was Col Jim Beckwith, 15th FG CO. Despite commanding the group through its transition to the P-51, its training for the VLR role and its difficult first fortnight on Iwo Jima, Beckwith would return home without completing a single mission over Japan. The same was not true for the other reassigned 15th FG leaders – deputy group commander Emmett Kearney, 45th FS CO Buck Snipes and 78th FS CO Jim Vande Hey – all of whom had not only earned membership to the 'Tokyo Club', but also had scored confirmed victories in the process.

Assigned as the new commanding officer of the 15th FG was Lt Col DeWitt Spain, who became available to move over from the 21st FG with the return of Col Ken Powell from convalescence in Hawaii. Powell's deputy would be Lt Col Charles E Taylor, who was an old 'Pineapple' returning to the Pacific after a year of duty Stateside and a temporary assignment in England. Capt Art Bridge, another veteran of the Marshall Islands campaign, moved up to take command of the 45th FS, and Maj Jim Tapp took over the reins of the 78th FS.

Following the fiasco over Kyushu, VII Fighter Command put on another airfield sweep for 19 April, with Atsugi Naval Airfield near Tokyo as the primary objective. This time, the planning was better, the target was more lucrative and the results would be excellent. The 21st FG, assigned the attack role with the 15th FG providing top cover, swept across Atsugi on the deck and caught the Japanese by surprise. The base was crowded with an estimated 150 to 200 parked aircraft, and the Mustang pilots tore into them, claiming 14 destroyed and another 53 damaged. Pulling off of

Working on the line could be dangerous. A battle-damaged B-29 of the 504th BG crash-landed at South Field on 24 April, wiping our four P-51s of the 15th FG, including Col. Jim Beckwith's *Squirt*. A fire broke out following the accident, but all members of the B-29 crew got out safely and no groundcrewmen were hurt. Note how the men visible in this view are taking cover because ammunition in the burning B-29 has begun to cook off (*Leo Hines*)

15th FG CO Col James O Beckwith named all of his assigned aircraft throughout the war after his daughter, whose nickname was 'Squirt'. After his first Mustang 44-63423 was wrecked on 24 April (see page 64), he was assigned this P-51D (44-64015). The fighter was subsequently passed to Lt Col Jack Thomas, who was killed in it on 19 July 1945 (*John Googe*)

the target, the 46th and 72nd FSs came upon a flight of J1N1 Gekko twin-engined naval fighters and claimed nine destroyed and one damaged. Similarly, the 531st encountered a number of training aeroplanes flying near Atsugi and shot down several.

Two P-51s were lost in the strafing attack – 1Lt Thomas L Cole of the 46th FS was hit by ground fire and crashed to his death over Atsugi, while 1Lt Arthur R Beckington of the 531st FS was last seen with smoke pouring from his engine as he approached the Tama River. Beckington, on his first mission, was later learned to have been taken prisoner, making him the first of nine Iwo Jima-based fighter pilots to become PoWs. After the war ended, he was found by occupying troops in a Yokohama jail in emaciated condition and flown to San Francisco to recover his health. Not

As the strain of VLR operations began to wear on the 'Sun Setters', it became common practice to assign two pilots per aeroplane. That way, one pilot could fly while the other rested, and the Mustang stayed operational. *"Mary Alyce"* (44-63451) was shared by 1Lts Robert J Louwers and John E Montgomery III of the 46th FS. The fighter was named for Louwers' wife, but did she pose for the pin-up painting on the fuselage?! (*Bob Louwers*)

long after that, Beckington had a reunion with fellow 531st FS pilot Dave Scotford, who related their discussion;

'I asked Art if he knew how he was shot down. He replied that it was ground flak near Atsugi. He said he noticed his oil pressure was low and decided to try to get to the coast and find the rescue submarine, which would have been located about 20 miles offshore. However, his engine stopped and he bellied into a field before he could even make a turn to get to the sea. The plane ploughed across the field and came to a stop at the end of the field, with the tail up and nose in a ditch. Beckington's head hit the gunsight, but he got the canopy off and tried to get out of the cockpit, but had forgotten to release the seat belt. He fell back, got his seat belt off and rolled out of the cockpit to the ground.

'Immediately he was grabbed by some kids. Knowing that the P-51 was soon going to burn, Beckington dragged them away from the aeroplane. Just as he cleared the wing, the fighter exploded in flame, but he and his captors were not hurt.

'After staggering away, they were met by some policemen who took him to a Yokohama jail. Beckington was first faced in the jail by a number of policemen who took turns kicking him in the groin. He was put in a small cell and not given much to eat. He said he could occasionally hear the engines of American aeroplanes, and worried about us.

'After two months a few other American fighter pilots were brought to the jail. Several times Beckington was interrogated about the P-51, which was new to the Japanese. They had no idea what an expert they had – a fighter pilot who was a lifelong model aeroplane builder and aeronautical engineering student at MIT. The specifications he gave them were plausible, but bogus. Late in the war our intelligence picked up this information and relayed it to us. We found it funny, because it was close, but so wrong.'

Although caught by surprise, the Japanese were able to launch a number of fighters in opposition to the marauding Mustangs. The 15th FG encountered mostly J2M Raidens, a stubby but formidable naval fighter, claiming five destroyed and two damaged for no losses. Maj Jim Tapp, leading the 78th FS, nailed one of them for his aforementioned sixth victory. Also getting a victory that day was Capt F H 'Herb' Henderson of the 45th FS, a seasoned veteran of the Marshall Islands campaign, who gave this account;

'I was the leader of a flight that also consisted of John Kester, Don Statsmann and a fourth pilot who may have aborted on take-off. We were ready to return to Iwo Jima when I spotted two J2M "Jacks" headed toward the mainland. We gave chase, and the three of us took shots at the trailing "Jack". I made a pass on him, scoring hits, but had to break off because I overran him. Kester was next to score hits, but he too overran and had to break off. Statsmann finally finished him off. The "Jack" literally started coming apart and spun into the water. We split the credit three ways.

'I still had the lead "Jack" in sight, and went after him. When I got in range I began spraying him. He headed for the deck, making violent turns right and left. I managed to catch him in a steep turn to the right and got fatal hits on him. My gun camera confirmed the kill. We were over land by that time.

'As I broke off, I found that I was alone. I had lost both my wingman and element leader in the chase. As a matter of fact, I did not see another Mustang anywhere. The en route weather to Iwo became so bad I was flying on instruments. I broke into a clear space and spotted a B-29. I closed on him and asked if he would drop me off at Iwo. I flew his wing through weather until he let down and pointed to the left, and there was Iwo. What a great group the B-29 guys were.'

The next VLR mission was a fighter sweep on 22 April targeting Suzuka airfield at Nagoya – the Mustangs' first visit to this area south of Tokyo. After their success at Atsugi, the Mustang pilots looked forward to another fruitful mission, and that's what they got. The claims were 14 aircraft destroyed on the ground and nine more in the air, for the loss of one pilot. Maj Fred Shirley of the 46th FS took the scoring lead in the 21st FG, shooting down two Raidens to bring his total to four confirmed aerial victories. He was not fated to get a fifth kill and make ace, however, as weather conditions hampered operations and precluded any further scoring by VII Fighter Command over the next month, by which time Shirley had completed his tour and returned to the US.

Bad weather would cost VII Fighter Command six pilots on 26 April, when the P-51s escorted B-29s to Kanoya, and one more on the 30 April escort against Tachikawa Army Air Arsenal. On the latter mission, 1Lt John Galbraith was leading the submarine cover flight of the 531st FS – normally a boring job, as the rescue submarines were rarely threatened, but not on this day. He filed this report;

Maj Fred A Shirley, 46th FS CO, had flown 16 missions with the 45th FS in the Marshalls campaign without scoring a victory, but he made up for lost time when he got to Iwo Jima. He shot down two J2M Raidens on 22 April 1945 to bring his total to four victories, before returning to the US a few weeks later. His *Miss Gene V* (44-63775), named for his future wife, was transferred in June to the 72nd FS and was lost on 1 August with Flt Off Philip B Ingalls at the controls (*Bob Louwers*)

67

'At 1200 hrs the submarine called our escort "Superdumbo" (a Navy PBY patrol aeroplane) and said, "Send your chickens against three picket boats ahead of me". I acknowledged his call and started a climb to the cloud base, which was at 2300 ft, and was about 4000 ft thick. A haze hung below the clouds and offered concealment. The three boats were in line abreast, approximately a quarter-of-a-mile apart, heading for the submarine at maximum speed judging from their wakes. I

told my element leader, 1Lt Harry DeRieux, to take the boat on the left, while my wingman 1Lt Dale Meyer took the middle one and I went after the one on the extreme right.

'We all made a simultaneous attack from bow to stern, clearing the decks of all personnel. We immediately climbed up to 2000 ft and set up another pass. On the second pass, I noticed a long-barrelled gun of probably 20 mm size on the boat that I strafed. It was revolving freely on its mount. After observing this gun, I changed all my passes to rear-quarter attacks from "four" or "five o'clock". The stack and pilot house blanked out the possible fire from the gun at this angle, and I observed no return fire. We made from six to seven passes, each man alternating on every boat, leaving two boats dead in the water and burning fiercely. One boat was smoking slightly, but still moving aimlessly.

'We returned to the submarine and orbited, from where two large columns of white smoke could be seen rising from the burning ships. Within a few moments the sub told us to hit the third boat again, as he thought it was still coming. We went back and I looked it over – no signs of life were evident and black smoke was rising, but the prop was still churning, so we made two passes apiece on it. After this attack it stopped and began burning about the pilot house. I observed the other two at this time – ammunition was exploding on one, observed by the sub, which asked if a gun were firing. Both the other boats were burning from bow to stern and settling in the water. We returned to the sub, which submerged at 1238 hrs.'

It was a fitting end to the first month of VLR operations. The next three weeks would be less notable for operations than they were for the arrival of a third P-51 group on Iwo Jima.

MORE MUSTANGS JOIN THE FIGHT

On a sunny morning in early autumn 1944, Col Bryan B Harper welcomed Maj Malcolm C Watters into his office at 53rd FG headquarters on Page Field at Fort Myers, Florida. Harper, 33-year-old commander of the training unit, had just received news that he had been waiting for since the war began nearly three years earlier. A new fighter group, the 506th, was being formed for a combat assignment to provide Very Long Range escort in the Pacific Theatre, and Harper would be its

Col. Bryan B. Harper organized the 506th FG in Florida in October 1944, oversaw its training as the only P-51 unit trained specifically from formation for the VLR mission and served as its commanding officer through the end of the war. The men of the 506th revered Harper for his honesty, fairness and courage. (*Chet Raun*)

Left
Two P-51s were destroyed and one damaged in this 45th FS mishap. The accident occurred when the pilot of 44-63214 lost control and slid into *Foxy* (44-63474), which is obscured by the smoke, and then flipped over onto the wing of 44-63428. This view clearly shows the 45th FS markings – black-bordered green bands, which did not extend under the wing or tail surfaces (*Tom Ivie*)

The three original squadron commanders of the 506th FG go for a ride in a Jeep. They are, from left to right, Maj Harrison B Shipman (458th FS), Maj Thomas D DeJarnette (462nd FS) and Maj Malcolm C Watters (457th FS). Only DeJarnette had combat experience prior to joining the group, having flown P-39s in New Guinea during 1942-43. Shipman and Watters came from Air Training Command (*Harrison Shipman*)

commanding officer. Now he needed a solid core of subordinates to help train and lead the new group, which was why he had summoned Watters to his office.

Harper was well acquainted with Maj Watters, who had served in the 53rd FG during its deployment to the Panama Canal Zone earlier in the war, and now commanded one of its training squadrons. Like Harper, he had been hoping for a combat assignment for a long time, and now the colonel offered him a job as a squadron commander in his 506th FG. Watters was intrigued, and asked Harper who was in the group. 'If you say "yes", it's you and me!' Harper replied.

Watters readily accepted command of the 457th FS, and the new VLR group was on its way. The 506th was activated on 21 October 1944 and set up shop at Lakeland Army Air Field, Florida. Soon pilots, mechanics, armourers and support personnel began arriving from all over. Harper tapped another of his squadron commanders at Fort Myers, Maj Harrison B Shipman, to command the 458th FS. Maj Thomas D DeJarnette, commanding the 462nd FS, was a combat veteran, as were the deputy group CO, Lt Col Harvey J Scandrett, and the group operations officer, Maj Harley Brown. All three pilots had flown P-39s during 1942-43 in New Guinea, and Scandrett had one confirmed kill to his credit.

Many of the other pilots in the 506th were escapees from Air Training Command, with long flying résumés and great skill, but no combat experience. Typical of these men was 1Lt Wesley A Murphey Jr, who had a total of 996.20 hours of flying time when he made his first Mustang flight at Lakeland on 3 November 1944;

'I was flying P-39s at Venice, Florida, in August 1943. About the end of the month, because of maintenance problems and a lack of flyable aircraft, a group of us were transferred to a P-47 Replacement Training Unit at

1Lt Wes Murphey was one of the many pilots who joined the 506th FG with extensive flying experience garnered during stateside assignments. Murphey had a total of 996.20 hours of flight time when he was assigned to the 457th FS at Lakeland, Florida, in October 1944. He would fly *"NIP 'NOCKER"* (44-63291) on 11 combat missions, claiming one confirmed victory and one aircraft damaged (*Lou Lascola*)

Fort Myers. After completing the 60-hour training course in this aeroplane, six of us were selected to remain at Fort Myers as instructors. Several months later I was appointed to the squadron gunnery officer's job. I completed the gunnery officer's course in P-47s at Matagorda, Texas, in April 1944. On 1 May our P-47s were transferred to II Fighter Command, and we received new P-40Ns in their place.

'Then in October our group commander, Col Harper, was selected to organise a long-range fighter group for escort duty in the Pacific Theatre. We were to train in P-51s at Lakeland. Chauncey Newcomb, Jack Folsom, John Benbow, Daun Anthony, Vance Middaugh, myself and several other pilots from Fort Myers went to Lakeland with Col Harper. The 506th FG was formed, and I wound up in the 457th FS as assistant flight commander of "C" or "Blue Flight" under Jack Folsom. Our squadron commander was Malcolm Watters.

Cpl Duane Marshall of the 462nd FS takes a break during training in Florida in 1944 to display a Browning M-2 0.50-cal machine gun he has been servicing. The Mustang behind him is a well used P-51A. The 506th FG used every model of Mustang while it was training for the VLR mission (*Duane Marshall*)

P-51B 43-12116 was one of the Mustangs that the 506th FG flew on training missions in the southeastern US prior to deploying to Iwo Jima (*Irv Howard*)

'We started flying around 1 November, and had all models of P-51s – As, Bs, Cs, Ds and Ks. One night we were taking off to fly a group formation – all three squadrons. I had an old A-model, and shortly after take-off it had an engine fire. By the time I got back on the ground and the crash crew had put the fire out, the aeroplane was damaged beyond repair. We finished training in early February 1945.'

The training regimen centred on learning cruise control techniques that would produce maximum range from the Mustangs. It also included practice scrambles, assembly and landing procedures, escort formations, aerial gunnery and bombing practice, and an occasional dogfight. A month after the 506th started flying, the USAAF produced document 50-100, which was the training directive for Very Long Range operations. Fortunately, the group had already met many of the requirements by then, two glaring exceptions being instrument flying and rocket firing. The final weeks of training were concentrated on mastering those tasks.

The day that the Marines landed on Iwo Jima, 19 February 1945, found the air echelon of the 506th FG aboard a train bound for California, where the aircraft carrier USS *Kalinin Bay* was waiting to carry them across the Pacific. On 6 March, when VII Fighter Command Mustangs first landed on Iwo Jima, the 506th was enjoying a night of liberty in Honolulu prior to setting sail for Guam the next day.

The ship delivered the 506th to Guam on 17 March, and a week later the pilots flew their new P-51D-20s to Tinian. There they would stay for seven weeks, flying combat air patrols and practice missions while the field engineers on Iwo Jima prepared a new base for them at the northern end of the island. At some point, it was decided that the 506th FG would be assigned to the Twentieth Air Force, which would 'loan' the unit to 'Mickey' Moore's VII Fighter Command.

Meanwhile, the ground echelon of the 506th was proceeding to Iwo Jima aboard the MV *Bloemfontein*, which, incidentally, was the same ship that had carried many of the American Volunteer Group personnel to

The *MV Bloemfontein*, which carried the ground echelon of the 506th FG from San Francisco to the combat zone, had been serving as a troop transport throughout the war. In fact, this same vessel transported members of the American Volunteer Group from the West Coast to Rangoon, Burma, to fly for China in 1941 (*Bob Torgerson*)

Burma back in 1941. The ship delivered the men of the 506th FG to Iwo on 25 April, and they set to work preparing North Field for the arrival of the group's pilots and aeroplanes. 1Lt Proctor Thompson, a ground echelon officer assigned to group headquarters, wrote this account of the 506th's first weeks on Iwo;

'The dead Japs, the vegetation, dud shells, mines, rocks and caves had been cleared by the 81st Service Group bulldozers. The night found us cold, uncomfortable, apprehensive. In the next few days, the setting up of our temporary area was nothing but indescribable confusion. Pup tents, wall tents, pyramidal tents went up willy-nilly, helter-skelter, in no semblance of order. But toward the end of the month the confusion diminished. Men were housed in 12-man squad tents, and officers moved up the slope to a cleared area below Bloody Ridge. The more technically minded men scraped out foxholes and slit trenches.

'Meals were unadulterated C and K Rations, mostly C, which was substantial enough, but a trifle high in beans and extremely monotonous after the first few days. The first few nights were hideous, with apprehension and rifle fire squeezed off by trigger-happy guards. Men crept to the latrine only when pangs from their bulging bladders overcame their better judgment. One or two Japs were sighted on Bloody Ridge during the third night, but gradually things quieted down.

'From this time forward, the job was organisation of the living areas, mess facilities and the line. Construction of our airfield – Strip No 3, or North Field – begun by the Seabees under Jap fire, was near complete by 5 May. The strip was dusty, bumpy and, by courtesy of Lucifer, sulphur-steam heated, but it was usable. The air echelon did not arrive on schedule because of dirty weather between Iwo and Tinian, but finally the skies cleared, and the aeroplanes came in. It was 11 May 1945.'

The weather closed back in, and it was not until 18 May that the 506th could fly its first combat mission – an obligatory strike on Chichi Jima by the 462nd FS. The other two squadrons followed shortly with their own missions to Chichi, and then – after several weather delays – the 506th FG was ready to fly its first mission to Japan.

With Col Harper leading, the group set out on 28 May for its first VLR mission – a fighter sweep and strike against Kasumigaura Airfield, northeast of Tokyo. This target was farther north than any of the previous VLR missions had ventured, but the mission went off without a hitch. The 457th FS attacked first, diving and strafing from 8000 ft down to 4500 ft so as to suppress the flak installations. The 462nd FS and then the 458th FS followed, attacking airfield installations in roughly line-abreast formations against moderate and inaccurate ground fire. Following VII Fighter Command policy, the 506th FG made one pass and then withdrew, leaving seven large fires burning on the field. One Mustang reported minor damage from ground fire in return.

As the 458th FS pulled off the target, a radial-engined enemy fighter attempted to make a pass at 1Lt Quarterman Lee of 'Yellow Flight'. Capt Francis C Carmody, leading 'Blue Flight', shot the aeroplane down as it broke off at low altitude in a slow chandelle to score the 506th FG's first confirmed aerial victory. Moments later about six Ki-44 Shokis made an ineffective run against 'Blue' and 'Green' flights of the 457th FS, the Mustang pilots claiming hits on two of them – Maj Watters was subsequently credited with one confirmed victory.

As the fighters withdrew southward toward the Rally Point, they strafed several other airfields along the route. The 462nd attacked Iba, and in doing so Capt Kensley M Miller was hit by ground fire and crashed to his death. This was a big loss to the squadron, as Miller was a combat veteran

When the 506th FG arrived on Tinian in late March 1945, the pilots and crew chiefs immediately got busy painting striped tail markings on their new P-51s. The green stripes of the 457th FS are visible on the rudder of P-51D 44-72599. The diary of Capt John Benbow recorded how it took three days to complete the painting of his flight's Mustangs – one reason why the squadrons were happy to convert to solid coloured tails later on (*Larry Dolan*)

1Lt Quarterman Lee Jr's child was obviously the inspiration for the name and artwork on his 458th FS P-51D *"Little Que"* (44-72606). Lee had a close call on the 506th FG's first VLR mission, on 28 May 1945, when an enemy fighter made a pass at him. The Japanese aircraft was shot down by Capt Francis C Carmody, leading 'Blue Flight', for the group's first confirmed aerial victory (*Tom Ivie*)

who had flown 80 missions in the MTO on P-40s. The 506th had lost several pilots previously in crashes, but Miller was the group's first loss due to enemy action.

STRONG END TO A SOGGY MONTH

Bad weather – including a typhoon that blew across Iwo Jima in mid-month – hindered VII Fighter Command operations for much of May. On the 17th of the month, while the 15th FG was bogged down in the mud at Airfield No 1, the 21st FG mounted a fruitful strafing mission against Atsugi Naval Airfield, but lost four pilots in the process. Then two more missions, on 19 and 24 May, had to be aborted due to weather.

By this time further changes were occurring in the leadership ranks of VII Fighter Command as more veteran pilots earned their tickets home. In the 15th FG, CO DeWitt Spain was replaced by Lt Col Julian E 'Jack' Thomas, who was yet another old 'Pineapple' pilot.

Thomas, a survivor of the Pearl Harbor attack, had commanded the 45th FS throughout its highly successful campaign in the Marshall Islands, and was returning to action after a frustrating year in Air Training Command. He was known as an especially aggressive pilot, and as an officer who put great stock in the military philosophy that commanders must 'lead from the front'. In the 47th FS, Maj John Piper handed over command to his operations officer, Capt Ed Markham.

Two squadron commanders in the 21st FG, Maj Fred Shirley in the 46th and Maj Paul Imig in the 72nd, headed for home at this time and turned their units over to Majs Benjamin C Warren and James C Van Nada, respectively. In a few weeks, Col Ken Powell would get his orders home as well, turning command of the 21st FG over to Lt Col Charlie Taylor.

Another new face with a strong combat resumé was Lt Col John W Mitchell of VII Fighter Command staff. Already an ace with eight victories scored in the South Pacific during 1942-43, he was best known for having led the P-38 mission that shot down Adm Isoroku Yamamoto,

'Pineapple' pilot Julian E "Jack" Thomas, seen here as a major, commanded the 45th FS during the Marshall Islands campaign, completing 18 missions and earning a Distinguished Flying Cross. After a stateside leave and promotion to lieutenant colonel, he returned to action as commanding officer of the 15th FG on 15 May 1945. He named all his aeroplanes, including this P-40N, for his beloved wife Jickie (*Jack Lambert*)

1Lt Vic Kilkowski of the 46th FS poses with his trusty P-51D *Little MAGGIE* (44-63719), which was named in honour of his wife. A replacement pilot, Kilkowski joined the 46th FS a few days after the 26 March banzai raid, flew missions through to the end of the war and remained in the 21st FG until April 1946. He subsequently enjoyed a long career in the Maryland Air National Guard, retiring as a brigadier general (*Vic Kilkowski*)

VII Fighter Command Mustangs carried high-velocity aerial rockets on an Empire mission for the first time on 25 May 1945. Here, a crewman fills one of the 165-gallon drop tanks attached to P-51D '129' of the 78th FS. The extra weight and drag imposed by the rockets necessitated the use of oversized drop tanks to give the Mustangs the range they needed to complete the mission (*Bill Killion*)

architect of the Pearl Harbor attack. Mitchell wasted no time in getting himself assigned to fly missions with the 15th FG.

Finally, on 25 May the 15th and 21st FGs were able to sortie on a maximum effort mission against airfields in the Tokyo area. A heavy weather front reduced the force from 128 P-51s taking off, including spares, to just 67 reaching Japan.

The 15th FG, led by Lt Col Mitchell at the head of the 47th FS, hit several airfields, starting with Matsudo. The 47th FS arrived over the target at 500 ft and made a pass on a line of fighters, believed to be Ki-44s, getting hits on seven of them and leaving one on fire.

Next came the 78th FS, with Capt 'Todd' Moore leading. One flight of 78th FS Mustangs carried rockets on this mission – a first for VII Fighter Command – and was trailing. Because of the extra drag imposed by the six 5-inch high-velocity rockets carried under their wings, the four P-51s were equipped with 165-gallon drop tanks in place of the normal 110-gallon models to give them sufficient range to reach the target. Maj Jim Tapp and his wingman, 1Lt Phil Maher, fired their rockets successfully at two hangers on Matsudo Airfield, setting fire to both targets.

As Capt Moore pulled up from Matsudo, he spotted a formation of enemy fighters to the north and gave chase. Always aggressive, Moore flamed two A6M Zeros in the scrap that ensued, and the other 78th FS pilots claimed six more. Moore's two kills took his tally to six victories (including one scored with the 45th FS during the Marshall Islands campaign), thus making him the second VLR ace.

Tempering Moore's success, squadronmate 1Lt Robert W Williams was shot down and taken prisoner. He later died of his wounds.

The 21st FG, led by Lt Col Taylor, attacked Tokorozawa Airfield west of Tokyo and destroyed eight aircraft, but did not encounter any aerial opposition. However, Taylor's Mustang was subsequently badly hit by return fire when he strafed a tug boat just off the coast. He bailed out close by the rescue submarine USS *Razorback* and was quickly hauled aboard, wet, but unhurt.

Shortly afterwards, the engine in 1Lt Walt Kreimann's P-51 caught fire about 375 miles short of Iwo Jima, and the 78th FS pilot, too, jumped out. Although his body and his parachute were partially burned, Kreimann survived the jump and was picked up by another submarine, USS *Tigrone*. Both men returned to Iwo Jima when the submarines completed their patrols, but Kreimann spent the next two-and-a-half months in the hospital recovering from his burns.

Groundcrews were the glue that held the 'Sun Setters'' operations together. Here, 15 crew chiefs of the 78th FS pose with P-51D *Jeanne VIII* (44-63973), assigned to squadron commander Maj Jim Vande Hey. The aeroplane's crew chief, SSgt Matthew Emberson, is standing third from the left in the top row (*Matthew Emberson*)

Maj R W 'Todd' Moore of the 78th FS became the second 'Sun Setters' ace when he shot down two A6M Zeros on 25 May to bring his victory total to six. Moore, seen here in his 78th FS P-51D, transferred to the 45th FS a few days later and continued to score, finishing the war as the top ace of VII Fighter Command with 12 confirmed victories (*Tom Ivie*)

Two blue-striped Mustangs of the 46th FS fly in formation. The aircraft closest to the camera is *Pat-Riot* (44-63737), which carried its name on the port side only. Flying wing is Capt Charles O 'Drip' Rainwater in his *Drip n Dick* (44-63960). Rainwater scored the first of his three confirmed victories on 29 May (*Tom Ivie*)

The XXI Bomber Command mission on 29 May would be the first strike of any kind against Japan's great port on Tokyo Bay, Yokohama. This was to be a daylight incendiary raid on the city's industrial area, with 101 Mustangs of the 15th and 21st FGs returning to the escort role to provide protection for 454 bombers from all four of Gen LeMay's B-29 wings. The stage was set for what would turn out to be one biggest air battles of the entire Pacific War – and the most fruitful day for aerial victories that VII Fighter Command ever had.

The P-51s took off just at 0630 hrs and headed north, dropping to 2000 ft at one point to pass under a weather front, before climbing to their escort altitude of 20,000 ft for rendezvous with the B-29s. The Mustangs reached the Departure Point, which was landfall, ahead of the B-29s, and made two orbits before the bombers arrived at 1000 hrs. Then the fighter flights spread to cover the bombers, and the massive formation headed east from Mt Fuji on a vector toward the target. The Japanese defences were ready and waiting. Soon the sky was dotted with bursting flak and small formations of intercepting fighters.

Twin-mounted 20 mm anti-aircraft guns are pointed skyward in this view of South Field, with Mt Suribachi in the background. On the field are P-51Ds of the 78th (closest) and 45th FSs, 73rd BW B-29s and P-61s of the 548th or 549th NFSs (*Leo Hines*)

It was time for the P-51 pilots to get to work, and they did so with a vengeance. Within minutes, Mustangs were engaging Japanese fighters at points all around the B-29 formations.

Capt R W 'Todd' Moore was leading a 45th FS flight covering the lead section of B-29s, having transferred from the 78th FS just a day or two prior. He spotted three J2M Raidens at 'ten o'clock high' and gave chase, instructing his second element to attack the No 3 Raiden while he went after the leader.

Moore fired a deflection shot into the lead aeroplane and saw immediate hits, followed by the pilot bailing out. The No 2 Raiden peeled off into a steep dive, and Moore followed. His Mustang quickly overtook the Japanese fighter, and he fired a telling burst from a range of 300 yards that sent it crashing to the ground.

Reforming his flight, Moore patrolled along the bomber stream for several minutes before spotting two N1K Shidens circling over Yokohoma and giving chase. One Shiden dove away as Moore attempted to attack, while the other approached his Mustang from behind. The Mustang pilot circled tightly with this fighter and eventually got behind it, allowing him to fire a short burst into its wing. A second burst hit the Japanese fighter squarely, and its pilot bailed out. Sadly, a lone A6M attacked Moore's flight as they were withdrawing toward the Rally Point and shot down his wingman, 2Lt Rufus S Moore.

'Todd' Moore's three kills were two better than Jim Tapp of the 78th FS scored during the mission, allowing Moore to pass his rival as the leading ace of VII Fighter Command with nine confirmed victories. He never relinquished the title.

Overall, the Mustang pilots tallied 28 confirmed victories for the loss of one pilot and three P-51s, making 29 May 1945 the most successful VII Fighter Command mission of them all. The next Empire mission would turn out far differently for the 'Sun Setters'.

In late May 1945, some of the longest-serving pilots of VII Fighter Command began receiving orders sending them home to the US. Two of the first to go were Maj Fred Shirley (right) and Capt Bill Higgins (seated in the Jeep) of the 46th FS. Both had flown in the Marshall Islands campaign of 1943-44. Here, they get the welcome news from Col Ken Powell, 21st FG commander, as 1Lt Louis Gelbrick (left) looks on (*Jerry Nolin*)

THE SETTING SUN

The end of May 1945 found the 'Sun Setters' firmly established on Iwo Jima. After two-and-a-half months on the island, the men were now virtually free of the risk of running afoul of any remaining Japanese soldiers. Rumour had it that one of the few enemy holdouts had sneaked into an outdoor theatre area one night and watched part of a movie with his American enemies before someone spotted him and took him prisoner. A continuing hazard was mines, which remained sown about the island despite ongoing efforts to clear them.

Living conditions, though still spartan, were improving at the airfields. Soon, the officers would give up their tents for more sturdy metal Quonset huts, which would also replace kitchen tents and other canvas structures serving all ranks.

Sgt Chet Raun, a technician in the Photo Section of the 457th FS, recalled this period in a 2002 letter to the author;

'The first supply ship arrived around the middle of May, and we had our first hot meals since arriving. All was great except that the first meat was mutton from Australia. Our cooks tried every way known to them to cook the meat so it tasted like something other than candles. It finally occurred to someone that it would be better if the fat was removed before cooking. That helped, but to this day I do not eat mutton. The water problem was also solved by the arrival of a desalinisation unit.

Conditions improved for VII Fighter Command personnel on Iwo Jima as the summer of 1945 wore on, but they could never be described as luxurious. Here, 45th FS officers (from left to right) Capts William J Morrow and James W Haglund, 1Lt William M Parry, Maj David A Kyzer, 1Lt Joseph A Wanamaker and 2Lt Robert D Wray relax in the tent area at South Field (*Jill Wanamaker*)

Sgt Chet Raun takes a break from his duties in the 457th FS photo section to pose for his portrait next to the pin-up beauty adorning his squadron's P-51D-20 *Broadway Gal* (44-72570). The pilots who shared this plane were 1Lts Ralph Gardner and Chet Jatczak (*Chet Raun*)

'Bathing didn't occur for most of us until we found a hot thermal in the water just off the shore at the north end of the island. This was great until nurses arrived on the island, and such bathing became taboo. By this time, however, the squadron had set up salt water showers using water pumped in from the ocean.

'Aside from a machine to process 16 mm (gun camera) film, we had all the necessary equipment to operate the film lab. Our responsibilities included the maintenance of the gun cameras in the P-51s, bore-sighting the cameras so that they were synchronised with the aeroplane's machine guns, loading film into the cameras prior to a mission and retrieving it after the aeroplane's return. We had to send the 16 mm film to Saipan for processing. We also loaded the 16 mm film cassettes, processed still camera film and printed same, took pictures when requested and operated the 16 mm projectors. In most cases we had ample time to do our work, as long as we were kept posted on mission times.'

457th FS crew chief SSgt Lou Lascola listed his most memorable impressions of life on the island at this time;

'Nuisance air raids by the Japanese, just after bed time; getting into a fox hole with a corrugated tin cover; shooing off the gigantic green flies that fed on some not-yet-buried Japanese soldiers or US Marines; avoiding Sakai bottles in the caves because they could be booby-trapped; avoiding the ghoul "gold-diggers" that pestered us to see if we had any Jap gold teeth to sell; counting and identifying the aeroplanes returning from a mission, and saying a silent prayer. I cannot begin to explain the tremendous admiration and respect we felt toward these young fighter pilots.'

Sgt Irv Howard, an armourer in the 462nd FS, sits on the sandbags in front of his tent in the squadron housing area at North Field. The tents housed four to six men each. 'We were really crammed and totally isolated on that hellish island', Howard recalled (*Irv Howard*)

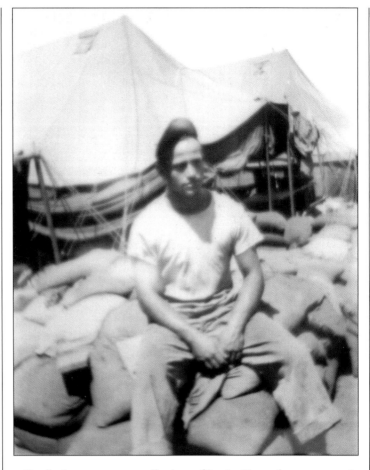

Finally, here are some recollections of Sgt Irv Howard, an armourer in the 462nd FS;

'Later on we lived in larger tents, which housed four to six men in each. We were really crammed and totally isolated on that hellish island. Some of the guys cracked with the loneliness and isolation, missing their wives, newly born offspring etc.

'I remember building our own washing machines – a wooden box containing a couple of boards, with a homemade windmill to move the boards up and back inside the box. In one area they constructed a latrine over a cave. After a few days several Japs came out of the cave and surrendered!'

Refinements in aircraft equipment and operational procedures were continuing as well. Experience had shown that the tail-warning radar sets installed in some of the P-51s were of little use in combat, so VII Fighter Command initiated a programme to remove them from all aircraft. On the positive side, AN/ARA-8 radio homing units, nicknamed 'Uncle Dog', were installed in the Mustangs to help the pilots find their way back to Iwo Jima. Problems with the SCR-522 and SCR-695 radio sets were also being addressed. For instance, the 531st FS Communication Section discovered that Iwo's fine volcanic dust was getting into the microphone relays and causing them to fail, so the technicians learned to keep a close eye on the units and replace them as needed.

New Mustangs arrived regularly to replace aircraft lost in combat or in accidents. Among these were some P-51D-25s, which were equipped with the new K-14 gyroscopic gunsight developed by the British to improve accuracy during deflection shooting. The K-14's gyroscope would measure the P-51's rate of turn and adjust the light projector accordingly to move the graticule on the reflector glass, thus displaying the angle of deflection required to hit the target. It required a little more dexterity on the part of the pilot, because he had to adjust the sight to the target aircraft's wingspan prior to making an attack. But the K-14 greatly improved shooting accuracy, particularly at long range and at deflection angles of 45 degrees or more.

The VLR mission procedures continued to be refined as well. For one thing, a senior 'Sun Setter' pilot was assigned to fly in each of the navigator B-29s that were used to lead the P-51 formations to Japan. These command pilots, supposedly well versed in the capabilities of the P-51 and the issues involved in safely completing a VLR mission, would call the shots in case the formation ran into bad weather or other problems while en route to the target.

For all these improvements, there was still no getting around the fact that flying an eight-hour mission in a Mustang, most of it over open sea, was an exhausting ordeal for the 'Sun Setter' pilots. One of the best descriptions of this was provided by Phil Alston, who flew eight VLR missions in the 457th FS, in response to a question by aviation historian Tom Ivie;

'It would take anywhere from two to three hours to get from Iwo Jima up to Japan. I don't know how anybody else felt, but my personal feelings were that I was awfully nervous, I don't mind admitting. And I was sitting

This training device was developed by TSgt Hubert Waugaman, with the help of three other communications technicians in the 458th FS, to teach pilots how to use the new 'Uncle Dog' radio homing controls. They installed a full P-51 cockpit inside a discarded drop tank so pilots could familiarise themselves with the location and proper use of the new equipment. Note the striped 458th FS tail markings (*Marie Waugaman*)

1Lt Philip S Alston (centre) poses with the 457th FS groundcrew of *LIL-TODDIE* (44-72557), which he shared with 1Lt John W Winnen. Barely visible in the photograph is nose art depicting a tipping shot glass pouring a bomb out of it. Winnen named the other side of the aeroplane *HEL-ETER* (*Phil Alston via Tom Ivie*)

there wondering about if I was going to be able to come through this mission. I mean, if I'd be able to get back to Iwo. They gave us a little lunch and a canteen of water to take with us, since the mission lasted all day. But I couldn't eat or drink anything the whole time going up there.

'We'd get up there and spend anywhere from half-an-hour to an hour over the target. Then we'd come off and rendezvous and start on the way back. Well, then you felt quite different. I mean it was just a really happy feeling that you'd have, and that's when I'd pull out my lunch and start eating it. I'd sometimes just sit there and sing – just really enjoy it – because I was happy to be alive and on my way back to Iwo.

'As far as the strain of over-the-water flights, well, we really didn't think too much about that. They gave us all the training on ditching the aeroplanes and survival in the dinghy out in the water – how to fish, what fish to eat and what not to eat. But it didn't really bother me too much flying over water, and that's what just about all our flying was. If anything went wrong, you go down in the water. But they had these air/sea rescue ships that you could navigate from one to the other.'

Extraordinary challenges such as those faced by the 'Sun Setters' bring out the best in some people, and one of them was Lt Col Joseph 'Smoky' Walther, VII Fighter Command flight surgeon. Here was a man completely devoted to the care and well being of 'Mickey' Moore's pilots – a trait he demonstrated more than once. The most extreme example of this came as the result of Brig Gen Moore's frustration over the loss of several pilots who were seen to bail out of their crippled P-51s successfully, yet who drowned before rescue crews could pick them up. He thought it would help if airborne paramedics were available to parachute to the rescue of downed pilots in the water.

When none of Walther's paramedics volunteered to make a test jump from a PBY to attempt rescuing a dummy, Walther agreed to do it himself. On the appointed day, the brave doctor leaped from the PBY, was knocked cold temporarily when one of the shroud lines of his parachute whacked him in the temple, and then nearly drowned when one of the two CO_2 bottles on his Mae West failed. After a miserable few hours in the water, during which time he did manage to 'rescue' the dummy, Walther was pulled aboard a destroyer and delivered back to Iwo.

The flying paramedic idea was abandoned as a result of the test, but two new procedures were identified that would help save pilots in the future. For one thing, all CO_2 bottle were tested, and it was found that half of them were defective. Also, a directive was published warning all pilots to put their hands over their temples after pulling the rip cord if they had to bail out.

Smoky Walther's other great contribution to the pilots was the facility that came to be called 'Ye Olde Iwo Jima Spa'. The doctor was becoming increasingly concerned about the condition of the Mustang pilots when they returned from the long VLR missions to Japan, many times so stiff and sore that they needed help from the crew chiefs just to climb out of their cockpits and down off the wing. Walther decided that what these boys needed at the end of a tough day in the cockpit was a steam bath and a rubdown.

As keeper of VII Fighter Command's medicinal liquor supply, Walther was able to barter with SeaBees on the island for their help in building the spa in a Quonset hut. Drilling into the ground, they were able to tap the nearly boiling water that lay just below the surface and direct it into 'catchalls' – large tubs normally used for collecting rain water. Pilots were

Pilots enjoy the steam baths and rubdown tables in 'Ye Olde Iwo Jima Spa' after a tiring VLR mission. The spa was the brainchild of Lt Col Joseph Walther, VII Fighter Command flight surgeon, who bribed some 133rd Naval Construction Battalion Seabees with mission liquor to convince them to build the facility. During the invasion of Iwo Jima just a few weeks earlier, the 133rd had suffered more men killed or wounded than any other Seabee battalion in any other engagement of the war (*Jerry Nolin*)

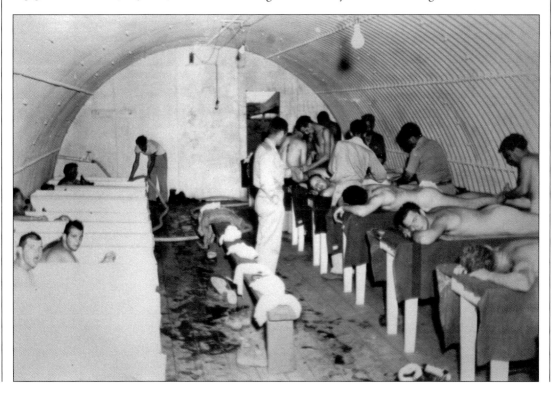

As more building materials arrived on Iwo, tents were replaced with more permanent structures such as the Quonset hut officers' club (left) and officers' quarters of the 78th FS at South Field. Note the classy stone fireplace chimney on the club building (*Bill Killion*)

welcome to drop their tired bodies into the tubs of hot water and enjoy a cold beer while their muscles relaxed. Then they could step across the aisle and lie face down on a table, where Walther's team of corpsmen gave them rubdowns. After a visit to the spa, pilots would begin to feel human again.

Despite all the improvements being made on Iwo Jima, one thing beyond repair was the weather. As had already become apparent in May, the northwest corner of the Pacific acts like a mixing bowl with the approach of the summer solstice, when cold weather blowing down off the Asian land mass runs smack into tropical air moving up from the south. The collision of weather systems creates violent storms, the likes of which no World War 2 fighter was designed to conquer.

If you asked the 'Sun Setter' pilots, most would tell you they considered the massive weather fronts they encountered on some Empire missions to be a more fearsome enemy than the Japanese defences opposing them on Honshu. The most extreme example of this occurred on 1 June 1945.

BLACK FRIDAY

Imagine you are a World War 2 American fighter pilot, headed north from Iwo Jima in your P-51D Mustang toward Japan. You're flying at 20,000 ft, loaded down with a full load of ammunition, internal fuel tanks filled to the brim and a 110-gallon drop tank hanging from each wing. Your speed is just a tad over 200 mph, and the Mustang is wallowing along like a truck. Yeah, you've got that big Merlin engine out front, but it's throttled back as far as you dare in order to save fuel for the long trip. Around you, there are forty-some guys from your fighter group in the same boat.

You peer into the distance ahead of you and see a long band of clouds rising from the horizon. 'How far away are those damned clouds?', you

462nd FS flight commander Capt John Findley pulls in close to the camera-ship to pose for a photograph in his P-51D *Pterodactyl* (44-72892). On 1 June 1945, Findley was assigned to fly as command pilot in one of the B-29 navigator aeroplanes leading VII Fighter Command Mustangs to Osaka. Unfortunately, the bomber had mechanical trouble and took off too late to help the P-51 pilots deal with the deadly storm they encountered (*Bill Ebersole*)

wonder. Minutes tick by and the cloud bank grows. Pretty soon you realise this is a major weather front. It rises up and up, topping out a good two miles above your present altitude. And it's spread out so wide that there's no chance of flying around it and still completing your mission. If you attempt to fly through, it's possible you will never come out the other side alive. But the B-29s are big enough to penetrate the front safely, and they're going to need your protection from enemy interceptors when they reach the target area.

This was the dilemma facing 148 'Sun Setter' pilots on 1 June as they set out on VLR Mission No 15 to provide escort for 400 B-29s assigned to attack Osaka. They had taken off in good weather at Iwo, clearing the island by 0710 hrs and proceeding to the rendezvous point at Kita Rocks, where they met the navigation B-29s that would lead them to the target. But by the time they reached about 370 miles away from base, everyone could see that a well-formed front, with angry cumulonimbus reaching to 30,000 ft, was blocking their path.

The navigator B-29s advised the three group leaders – Lt Col Jack Thomas, 15th FG, Maj Charles Chapin, 21st FG, and Lt Col Harvey Scandrett, 506th FG – to begin a climb over the front. But the call came too late, as the heavily loaded Mustangs were too close to the front to climb over it in the fleeting minutes before they would reach the clouds. Perhaps realising this, the B-29s continued flying straight and level, leading the P-51s directly into the storm.

Flying behind the formation in a B-29, with a bird's-eye view of the scene, was 462nd FS flight commander Capt John Findley. Just prior to going overseas, he had been pulled off terminal leave and sent through an accelerated weather programme at Bryan Field, Texas. On 1 June, he was assigned as the VII Fighter Command pilot in a B-29 that was supposed to go out 30 minutes ahead of the formation and scout the weather along the route to Japan. Findley's account of what happened during the fateful mission, compiled from a letter to the author and his mission report, is as follows;

'I attended the briefing the night before. The mission was ordered off against the wishes of the weather officer. At scheduled take-off, our B-29 developed engine trouble and we had to delay, so the next B-29 in line took our place. Unfortunately, the fighter pilot in that aeroplane had never had been on a Japan mission – he was new, and had only been to Chichi Jima. After the P-51s took off, we got the B-29 squared away and departed about 30 minutes behind the mission.

'I can still see in my mind's eye that endless line of cumulus clouds that marked the front, visible from about 100 miles away. We were aware of the tremendous build-up and began to climb. We were pushing the B-29, yet it appeared that no matter how fast we climbed, the tops of the clouds stayed with us, and the closer we got the more obvious it was we'd never get over the top. I remember looking at the rate-of-climb indicator, and it was at 1000 ft per minute. Still the clouds boiled up faster.

'Not long before we hit the front, the problem was obvious. The radio chatter was incessant and confused. We decided to go into the soup on the chance we might pick up an aeroplane or two that could fly wing on us until we could get them out. We did so, and by some good chance we ran into a hole among the clouds and saw several P-51s milling about in a circle. We dropped down, got them to tuck in tight, and led them out of the front and headed back toward Iwo.

'We decided to try this again, and found either the same hole or another one and circled in it waiting for survivors. We didn't find any. We headed for the deck in search of others. The front went down almost to water level. We searched, but found no one. Clearly the mission was over, and the remaining aeroplanes headed back to Iwo. We landed and learned quite a number of P-51s had not returned.'

The experience was even worse for the 'Sun Setter' pilots in the P-51s that penetrated the front. The report filed by the 458th FS after the mission described it this way;

'The front was entered between 10,000 and 11,000 ft. Visibility was zero, rain heavy, turbulence intense and violent. Groups, squadrons, flights and elements lost contact and scattered. Traffic on all radio channels was so heavy that communication was nearly impossible. Some pilots lost control completely, spun, recovered and spun again. Some recovered in time, some did not. Only 27 P-51s – none from the 458th – passed through the front and arrived over the target area.'

The experience of 72nd FS pilot 1Lt Leo Hines was typical. He described what happened to him;

'We headed into the soup. The confusion was unbelievable. Our formation dissolved from absolute necessity. I found myself alone, so I tacked onto a B-29 and flew formation with him until he indicated we were at 200 ft. I had seen the water a couple of times and figured I would be safer on my own. I picked up a reciprocal heading and broke into the clear on the Iwo side of the front. Maj Crim was in the vicinity, so I tacked onto his wing and returned to Iwo. God, what a mess.'

1Lt Leo M Hines of the 72nd FS was one of the lucky pilots who survived the disastrous 1 June 1945 mission, when the three groups of VII Fighter Command ran afoul of a massive weather front blocking their route to Tokyo and lost 24 pilots in the storm (*Leo Hines*)

Capt Francis Lee of the 462nd FS was one of the 27 pilots who made it through the front. He described his experience as follows;

'Tom DeJarnette was leading the squadron and I was leading the last eight aeroplanes. Tom called to tell us that in spite of "oranges being sour" (the code term for impassable weather), we were going to penetrate the front. We headed straight into the soup. He was interrupted by screams of pilots on the radio, aeroplanes bumping into one another, mid-air collisions, shouts of bailouts and pilots in spins. My radio then fell silent. I signalled to my pilots to go into the formation we had practiced at Lakeland – pull to the right ten degrees and make a shallow climb through the front. The cloud cover was so thick I could barely see my wingtips.

'After about 15 minutes of slow climbing, the sun was shining and I could see that my gun barrels were covered with ice. Then out of the blue came the call "Flight leader, what is your airspeed?" Startled, I looked to my right and there was my wingman, 1Lt Harley Meyer! He had stuck with me like a flea on a dog. We never saw another P-51 until we landed at Iwo seven hours later. I told Meyer that we would have to go down

462nd FS CO Maj Tom DeJarnette (top row second from left) and Lt Col Harley Brown (to his left) had flown P-39s together in New Guinea early in the war, and now shared P-51D *TALLAHASSEE LASSIE* (44-72547). Brown became deputy commander of the 506th FG after Lt Col Scandrett died on 1 June. Flanking the pilots are SSgt 'Pappy' Haynes (left), who was the fighter's crew chief, and Cpl Curt Gwaltney, assistant crew chief. In front are armourers and radio technicians from the 462nd (*Curt Gwaltney*)

1Lt Harley E Meyer (centre rear) of the 462nd FS stuck with element leader Capt Francis Lee through the storm on 1 June, and was one of the few pilots in his group to complete the mission to Osaka. Posing with Meyer here are , from left to right, fellow 462nd pilots Bob Graham, Ed Linfante, Harry Reese and Newt Milner (*Harry Reese*)

slowly to melt the ice. Down we went. As we were losing height, I felt the air turbulence of a four-engined aircraft. Sure enough, 15 minutes later I spotted a B-29 with a big "Z" on its tail. I called the B-29 and explained our situation to him. The B-29 pilot said he would make a single pass over the target and then help us with our problem. As he was going into his run, I spotted a Jap "Frank" (Ki-84) preparing to make a pass on the B-29. When the "Frank" spotted us, he took off. The B-29 made his bomb run, then picked us up on the other side of the target. So we tacked onto the bomber and headed for Iwo.

'When we landed at Iwo, all our friends climbed onto our wings and seemed genuinely happy to see us. It was great to be home. Then we got the bad news about the mission. The Good Lord really looked after us.'

In the 47th FS, the entire 'Yellow Flight' and half of 'Green Flight' simply disappeared – six pilots gone, which was the worst loss of any squadron in VII Fighter Command that day. But the 47th also had the distinction of scoring the only aerial victory of the mission. 1Lt Robert S Scamara wrote this account to the author 60 years later;

'I thought we would enter the clouds and in a few moments exit on the other side, but that wasn't the case. Imagine taking 65 or so P-51s in tight formation into a weather front with no sight distance, heavy rain and hard buffeting. Very afraid of hitting other aeroplanes in formation, I was one of the lucky ones and got through it okay. I don't know what happened to my wingman, who was a fill-in from the 45th FS (1Lt Lawrence Lortie, missing in action).

'I went on alone toward the target and got there while bombing was under way. I escorted several groups of B-29s over the target, which was one big fire with smoke up to 25,000 ft or more. Finally, I saw a two-engined "Nick" heading for the bombers. I dropped my external tanks and gave the P-51 full power to catch up to him. Then my engine stopped. A few terrified moments later, after I realised I hadn't switched to the internal tanks, the engine started up again. I caught the "Nick" easily. He probably never saw me, as he was intent on getting to the B-29s. My first burst, from the left side, knocked out his left engine and set him on fire. I coasted across behind him to his right side, giving him another burst just to get camera coverage of my kill, as I was alone and had no other witnesses. This was a must to get credit for a kill.

'After watching him spin down in flames, I looked around and found myself completely alone. I couldn't find the bombers. I tried to find our navigational B-29 that was at the Rally Point. He said he had to head back as he had two other P-51s and they were low on fuel, so he couldn't wait around any longer for me. He gave me his heading for Iwo. I didn't know

In addition to providing VII Fighter Command with air bases in range of Tokyo for its P-51s, Iwo Jima also served as a gas station for B-29s on their way home to their bases in the Marianas Islands. Here, B-29s of the 58th, 313th and 314th BWs fill the tarmac at one of the three Iwo Jima airfields (*Dave Scotford*)

if I was ahead, behind or parallel to him, but the heading got me home by myself – I hit Iwo on the nose. That's pretty good, finding a three-by-seven-mile island 650 miles away.

'The next day I went down to the flightline and asked about my film. The crew chief hesitated a little, then said, "Oh, haven't you heard? Your camera wasn't loaded properly, so no film". Our S-2 officer, Henry Sanders, said he would radio down to Bomber Command to see if any bomber crew had witnessed my kill. This was a long chance, but one crew reported a Jap aeroplane going down in flames, but didn't see who shot it down. Out of all the aeroplanes in the air that day, I was the only one to make a claim, so I got credit for my first kill.

'Later on, I received the Silver Star medal, pinned on my shirt by Gen Hap Arnold. I've never been sure that I earned it after seeing what the Marines had to go through taking Iwo Jima.'

The numbers tell the whole lesson of 1 June. Of the 24 Mustang pilots lost that day, not one went down as a result of enemy action – Mother Nature took them all. Among the pilots who did not come back were the formation leaders of the 21st FG, Maj Chapin, and the 506th FG, Lt Col Scandrett. John Findley recalled that an inquiry was held immediately after dinner that night, when it was discovered that the P-51 weather pilot in the lead B-29 had no combat experience. As a result, VII Fighter Command adopted a rule that in the future only combat-experienced 'Sun Setters' could fly as lead weather pilot.

The 45th FS got good news a week later when the submarine USS *Trutta* reported it had picked up one of the squadron's missing pilots, 1Lt Arthur A Burry. The engine in Burry's P-51 cut out temporarily while he was battling the storm, and he lost contact with his flight. He managed to

Lt Col Harvey Scandrett, deputy commander of the 506th FG, was killed flying P-51D *Madam Wham-Dam* (44-72607) while leading the group into the storm on 1 June. No trace of Scandrett, or the aeroplane, was ever found. The regular pilot of this fighter was Maj Harrison Shipman, CO of the 458th FS (*Bennett Commer*)

restart the engine and headed back to Iwo alone, but then he lost power for good and had to bail out about 275 miles north of home. After hitting the water, Burry had a little trouble getting out of his parachute harness, but within two minutes he was able to inflate his life raft and climb in. Then he settled down to await rescue.

Burry's first few days in the raft passed uneventfully, but on the night of June 5-6 he was caught in a storm that dumped him out of the raft several times and cost him his food supply, which was washed away. The next day he began having delusions – during one of them Burry believed he was at a party when a friend said he was sending a destroyer to pick him up. A report by the 45th FS intelligence officer finishes the story;

'Seventh Day – 7 June. The morning was clear and bright, and 1Lt Burry realised no destroyer was coming, and that he had been deluded the night before. Presently, he started hearing music, and distinct voices of people singing songs. Later, when the submarine picked him up, he was not delirious, but was somewhat incoherent. He seemed to expect the submarine, and took it as quite normal that he should be picked up. He was able to climb down the hatch without any help.'

1Lt Burry's rescue closed the books on Black Friday – the worst mission in the history of VII Fighter Command.

RUNNING UP THE SCORE

Bad weather hampered VLR operations throughout June, with just seven missions completed by the end of the month. After Black Friday, the 'Sun Setters' made another escort foray to Osaka on 7 June. Again, they encountered a weather front en route, but this time it did not amount to much, and neither did Japanese opposition over the target area. A flight

The top scorer on the 10 June escort to Tokyo was 1Lt Doyle T Brooks Jr of the 78th FS with two confirmed kills and one damaged. Here, he sits on the wing of his P-51D *Button-II* (44-63353). Later, the aeroplane carried the name *Jimmy*, as well as simplified unit markings (*Doyle Brooks*)

from the 462nd FS shot down an unidentified single-engined aircraft south of the city, and Maj 'Todd' Moore of the 45th FS destroyed a Ki-45 a few minutes later for his tenth victory.

The next scheduled mission was planned as a fighter sweep of Kagamigahara Airfield at Nagoya on 8 June, but the formation encountered a huge front about an hour after taking off and turned around to come home. Conditions were better the following day, and the mission was completed, with the 21st FG registering aerial claims of one probable and two damaged, plus seven ground kills. Two P-51s were lost to flak in the target area, and a third went down about ten miles from Iwo Jima, its pilot being quickly rescued.

The weather continued to cooperate on 10 June, when 107 Mustangs of the 15th and 506th FGs escorted B-29s to the Tokyo area. This time the Japanese put up an estimated 100 fighters in opposition, but their tactics were ineffective, and succeeded only in giving the P-51 pilots something to do. The result was a lopsided victory for the 'Sun Setters' – scores of 24 confirmed destroyed, 4 probably destroyed and seven damaged for no losses. Perhaps more importantly, no B-29s were lost either.

The top scorer on 10 June was 1Lt Doyle T Brooks Jr of the 78th FS with two confirmed kills and one damaged. This is how he recalled the mission;

'My flight leader had to abort during the VLR, and another pilot took his place. I remember looking down and seeing a Zero, and then calling "Let's go get him" over the radio. I dropped down to 5000 ft, and my aeroplane started porpoising due to excessive speed. I cut the throttle, reached down and put my pipper on top of the Zero's tail and fired. Smoke came out of his wing roots, and then I saw the Zero's pilot opening

The mix of squadron markings in the 458th FS is clearly visible in this photograph. In the foreground is *The Boll Weevil* (44-72558), flown by 1Lt Ben Commer. This aeroplane, which Commer shared with 1Lt Henry Seegers, was named *A Neat Package* on the other side of its nose. In the background is Capt Peter Nowick's P-51D 44-72970 in which the squadron operations officer scored two confirmed victories on 10 June (*Bennett Commer*)

his 'chute. I then looked over to my right and saw a second Zero. He was fishtailing in front of me to slow me down. He fell into a lazy barrel roll when I fired, and he too went down.'

After the mission, several 47th FS flight leaders reported having momentarily mistaken 506th FG Mustangs for Japanese aircraft because their tails appeared to be red (like the Ki-61s of the 244th Sentai) under certain light conditions, and the striped markings tended to camouflage the distinctive outline of the tail – one of the P-51's best recognition features. It may be that the 457th and 462nd FSs converted their tail markings to solid colours (green and yellow, respectively) as a result of this report.

Meanwhile, 462nd FS commander Maj Tom DeJarnette, who had shot down one Ki-61 that day, critiqued his squadron's performance during the mission as exhibiting 'poor air discipline'. Speaking with the authority only accorded to someone who had survived a full combat tour flying P-39 Airacobras over New Guinea earlier in the war, DeJarnette told his pilots that they had flown too close together, had been too individualistic and not watchful enough, and that the wingmen had not paid close enough attention to their leaders' flying. The squadron's pilots would have plenty of time to mull their commander's remarks, because the weather would scrub their next two missions.

Although the 21st FG pulled off a successful fighter strike against Tokyo on 11 June, the 15th and 506th FGs did not get another crack at the enemy for nearly two weeks.

On 23 June the weather finally improved, and 100 P-51s of the 15th and 506th FGs headed out for a fighter strike against airfields in the Tokyo area. Led by Lt Col Jack Thomas, the 15th FG was assigned to attack Shimodate and Kasumigaura airfields, while the 506th went after Hyakurigahara and Katori, with Maj Harrison Shipman leading. Another field day for the 'Sun Setters' was in the works.

1Lt Francis Clark of the 457th FS pauses in the cockpit of 44-72557 with the crew chief, SSgt Jaynes Gandy, behind him. The flaming nickname *Hel-Eter* combined the names of regular pilot John Winnen's wife Helen and son Peter. The origin of the *Lou-Flo* bunny artwork beneath the cockpit is unknown (*Tim Bivens*)

Maj Harrison B Shipman, 458th CO, led the 506th FG on the action-packed 23 June 1945 mission against Hyakurigahara Airfield. He initiated the strike with a diving rocket attack that destroyed a twin-engined aircraft on the field, before leading his squadron into the top-cover position in support of strafing runs made by the 462nd FS (*Harrison Shipman*)

This was the second 47th FS P-51D named *Hairless Joe* assigned to 1Lt Joseph P Brunette, who was a well-regarded flight commander in the unit. He wrecked the first (44-63467) in a take-off accident on 19 June. Its replacement (44-72223) carried the 47th FS badge and 'Dogpatch' name, but not the distinctive early yellow-edged black squadron markings (*John Googe*)

The 15th FG took off first and arrived at the Departure Point over Japan at 1300 hrs. Turning left, the formation proceeded above a deck of clouds for about four minutes, before the 47th FS was jumped by seven Ki-84 Hayates. The Japanese defenders made some moderately aggressive passes, but Lt Col Thomas and his wingman, Flt Off Fronnie A Jones Jr, were each able to shoot one down. After three-and-a-half years of war, Jack Thomas' determination to repay the enemy for the destruction he had witnessed during the Pearl Harbor attack had finally paid off.

While this was going on, the 78th FS made a strafing attack on Shimodate that netted three Ki-84s destroyed and three other aircraft damaged on the ground. Lt Col Thomas next led his group southeast toward Kasumigaura, and was jumped again about ten minutes later. This

time, 17 Ki-84s hit the 47th FS aggressively with an altitude advantage, breaking up the Americans' formation as a wild dogfight erupted and Japanese naval fighters also joined in.

The battle raged for about ten minutes, during which time the 15th FG pilots claimed an additional seven enemy aircraft destroyed, three probables and 14 damaged. The top scorer was 1Lt Bob Scamara of the 47th FS, with three confirmed kills. That made him the unit's leading scorer with four victories. Scamara would go on to complete 15 VLR missions by the end of the war – one of the few 'Sun Setters' to reach that total – but never got the opportunity to notch the fifth kill that would have made him an ace.

On the deficit side of the 15th FG's ledger, three P-51s were lost on 23 June. Two of the pilots bailed out over the sea and were rescued, but the third wasn't so lucky. During the fight, 1Lt Scamara's wingman, 1Lt John V Scanlan, was shot up by a Zero and bailed out over Chiba Peninsula, near Chosi Point. He was taken prisoner, but after the war it was learned that he had been executed while held as a PoW.

The 506th FG had an action-packed mission on 23 June as well. The group's navigator B-29s got slightly off course, and as a result the Mustangs made landfall north of the planned route and over an industrial area, where heavy and accurate flak greeted their arrival. The formation broke up, with the 457th FS proceeding to Mito South Airfield, which the pilots mistook for Naruto. There, the pilots made four strafing passes apiece before turning for home with claims of 11 aircraft destroyed on the ground.

The 458th FS, meanwhile, accompanied the 462nd FS to Hyakurigahara, where the former unit was assigned to hunt flak and

After more than three years at various airfields in the Hawaiian Islands, far from action on the battle front, it was only natural that the 47th FS would want to advertise the fact that it had at last reached the combat zone. The evil-looking bumble bee squadron insignia was also applied to the noses of many 47th FS P-51s (*John Googe*)

Mustangs of the 458th FS with solid and striped tails await their next mission at North Field. Identifiable P-51s (from the left) are '582' (44-72672), '565', '575' *My Madge* (44-72602), '593' (44-72803), '591' *Miss French* and '592' *Susie Kae* (*Harrison Shipman*)

Mice were a constant problem in the quarters on Iwo Jima, but the little critters met their match in 1Lt William G Ebersole, youngest pilot in the 462nd FS. When the men in his Quonset hut held a contest to see who could kill the most mice, and began keeping score, Ebersole developed a trigger for 1Lt Bob Graham's trap – known as the 'Graham Cracker' – and won hands down. Here, Ebersole (left) is presented with a medal honouring his success in front of the scoreboard (*Bill Ebersole*)

provide top cover for the latter. Led by Maj Shipman in a rocket-equipped P-51, the 458th pilots made a steep dive to the target and shot it up as best they could, before pulling back up to cover the attack by the 462nd FS. According to the mission report, Shipman's rockets destroyed a twin-engined aircraft on the field. One of the 462nd pilots, 1Lt William G Ebersole, wrote this account of his squadron's subsequent attack;

'I received credit for probably destroying one "Zeke" fighter on the ground (on 23 June). When we performed these strafing runs on airfields, four of our 16-aeroplane squadron would make a vertical dive on the target, firing at random to detract the ground fire, while the other 12

aeroplanes would dive down to tree-top level about 15 miles from the field and spread out in a horizontal line, with about 100 ft or so between the Mustangs. By staying in a horizontal line, we would not be in danger of shooting our own aeroplanes, but each pilot had very little room for manoeuvring, and had to take the targets in his particular path of flight.

'I still get goose bumps thinking back on the excitement of diving down from about 20,000 ft at close to full throttle, levelling out at tree-top height as one of a dozen aeroplanes lined up abreast, and racing across an airfield with guns blazing. We each had six 0.50-cal machine guns. Every fifth round of ammunition was a tracer bullet, with two incendiary and two armor-piercing bullets making up the other four of each five rounds. With the tracers ricocheting in all directions, the incendiary rounds exploding when they hit, explosions on the ground and a mass of return fire from enemy flak gunners, it would put any 4th of July finale to shame.'

After covering the 462nd FS strafing run, the 458th FS headed eastward toward the coast and began to climb, losing Maj Shipman's 'Blue Flight' in the process. The squadron's mission report detailed what happened next;

'Just west of Inubo Saki light, "Yellow Flight" saw eight bogies far below, flying a sloppy 3-1, 22 formation in trail, and in a climbing turn to the left. "Yellow Flight" bounced from 13,000 ft and drove in from above at "seven o'clock". The four trailing Zekes caught the attack. 1Lt (Harold) Davidson flamed one after a heavy burst in the cockpit. 1Lt (Evan) Stuart burned another. One enemy aircraft pulled up and out in a high roll, above Stuart. 1Lt (Roy) Kempert, "Yellow 2", nosed up, fired and got heavy strikes. The "Zeke" broke down and out, spun and trailed smoke. Kempert followed, firing. Finally he broke off and climbed almost

1Lt Evan Stuart, assistant operations officer of the 506th FG, was credited with two A6M Zeros confirmed destroyed in the air, one probable and one damaged on 23 June while flying with the 458th FS. The odd black marks in the picture are flaws in the original photo, not markings or damage on his P-51D *Precious Betty* (*Bennett Commer*)

vertically to rejoin. Another "Zeke" was starting down, and Kempert was forced to dive away. The "Zeke" did not follow through.

'1Lt (Jack) Kelsey, "Blue 3", with "Blue 4", was proceeding to the Rally Point when he saw the fight. He arrived in time to force a break from the enemy aircraft that had hovered above 1Lt Kempert after chasing 1Lt Davidson. The enemy aircraft dove away from 1Lt Kelsey, then chandelled and was hit hard as he did. He burned. The Zeke Kempert had originally fired at was, when last seen by Kelsey, in a tight spin, blazing.

'Meanwhile, 1Lt Davidson broke upward after his first pass and made a second run on the lead four enemy aircraft. He got strikes on the left wingman, then turned and looked down the gun barrels of a "Zeke" coming in high at "seven o'clock". Davidson snapped under and broke down and out. This "Zeke" is the same one credited above to 1Lt Kelsey.

'1Lt Stuart was, in the interim, making high wingovers into and out of the melee. On his second pass, he made strikes on an enemy aircraft in the first flight of four and then pulled up and knocked pieces off the tail of another diving in from "two o'clock high". He recovered, made another run and got strikes on another enemy aircraft. On his last pass, Stuart hit another "Zeke" in the wing, and then saw an enemy aircraft boring in from "five o'clock", firing, so he broke down and out in a spiral dive.

'"Red" and "Green Flights" were meanwhile heading about 270 degrees northwest of Inubo Saki light when four "Jacks" in box-four formation were called in at "ten o'clock low". The enemy aircraft were outnumbered and immediately dived for cloud cover. They did not reach it. "Red 1", Capt (J B) Baker, ran a burst into the tail of the fourth enemy aircraft, which chandelled tightly, caught Baker's second burst fairly in the cockpit and centre section and began to burn. 1Lt (Vance) Middaugh, "Red 3",

SSgt C L Hagerty (crew chief) and Capt J B Baker Jr (pilot) pose on the wing of their 458th FS P-51D *Delta Queen* (44-72591). They made a good team, as Baker shot down a Ki-44 Shoki on 23 June and followed up that success with a J2M Raiden probably destroyed on 6 July just east of Kashiwa (*Bennett Commer*)

1Lt Vance A Middaugh of the 458th FS was another pilot who made his mark during the 23 June mission, shooting down a Ki-44 Shoki for his only confirmed victory of the war. His P-51D was named *Bakersfield Baroness*, and it featured his squadron's dark blue striped tail markings (*Bennett Commer*)

shot and smoked the No 3 "Jack", which began to trail a small fire from its engine. 1Lt (Norman) Dostal saw this aircraft hit the ground and explode.

'1Lt (Max) Ruble, leading "Green Flight", crossed from the inside of the attack over "Red Flight" and put a burst into the belly of the second enemy aircraft, which broke right. Ruble pulled through to a 20-30 degree deflection, fired and set the "Jack" alight. The pilot jettisoned his canopy and rolled onto the wing while his aeroplane was still taking strikes. As Ruble ceased firing, the pilot opened his parachute. 1Lt (Wilhelm) Peterson, flying on Ruble's left wing, was unable to dodge and chopped the 'chute to bits with his propeller.

'"Green 3", 1Lt (Frank) Wheeler, crossed with his leader and opened fire on the flight leader. The "Jack" caught fire and the pilot bailed out.

The Japanese flag marking 1Lt Max E Ruble's confirmed victory over a J2M Raiden on 23 June is barely visible in this photograph of his 458th FS P-51D *Little One* (44-72612). Ruble shared the aeroplane with 1Lt Francis J Pilecki, who named it *The Fetter Moichant* in his native 'Connecticut-ese' on the starboard side (*Caren Krupinski*)

1Lt (G B) Lambert, forced out of position by the last crossover, swung wide to the right. he turned back and suddenly saw a "Jack" sitting ahead of him. He followed the enemy aircraft up to 1000-2000 ft, firing, and saw strikes and drew smoke. When last seen, the "Jack" was still smoking and in a split-S at about 1000 ft.'

All told, the 458th FS was credited with a score of ten destroyed, two probables and one damaged for the mission, with no losses. This was the 'Sun Setters' deepest penetration into enemy territory to date. The last Mustang returning to Iwo, flown by 1Lt William T Moore of the 457th FS, landed after bottom-numbing eight hours and 20 minutes in the air, setting a new record for VII Fighter Command.

The next mission, on 26 June, was an escort by all three VII Fighter Command fighter groups to Nagoya. Flak over the target was typically heavy, but few Japanese fighters rose to intercept the Americans. The 'Sun Setters' registered just two confirmed victories, but one of them was notable because it was the first kill in more than two years for Lt Col John Mitchell, who led the 15th FG that day. His wingman, 2Lt Doug Reese of the 45th FS, wrote this account;

'An aeroplane speeding toward us was aimed directly at Lt Col Mitchell. When two aeroplanes are coming together at speeds of over 200 mph, events happen fast. In your mind, however, everything is in slow motion. It was a Japanese aeroplane we had designated as a "Tony". The "Tony" had an inline engine, as did our Mustangs. The colonel thought it was one of our Mustangs, and he banked his aeroplane right out of the path of the

2Lt C Douglas Reese of the 45th FS was assigned *SAN ANTONIO ROSE* after his original Mustang was lost by another pilot. Although Reese thought the name of his new aeroplane was corny, he had good success with it, scoring single confirmed victories on 26 June and again on 8 July (*Doug Reese*)

Maj Harry C Crim Jr, 531st FS CO, scored his sixth, and last, confirmed victory during the 6 July fighter strike against airfields in the Tokyo area. Aerial opposition was light that day, with just nine enemy fighters encountered – Crim's kill was the only one claimed by the 'Sun Setters', along with six damaged. Here, crew chief Sgt Stanley McCarro poses in the cockpit of Crim's *My Achin!* (44-73623) (*Harry Crim via Tom Ivie*)

"Tony". I knew it was not a Mustang because of the dihedral of the wings. The six 0.50-cal machine guns in the wings of my Mustang were adjusted to converge 150 to 300 yards in front of the aeroplane. When the rounds meet at whatever distance, the fire will tear a hole in any aircraft. I started firing short bursts, counting on this fact to destroy the "Tony" before if got to me. It did not happen.

'At the last moment, the "Tony" became vulnerable as it started to pull up, and I saw strikes on his engine and puffs of smoke and flame. On the radio someone said, "He bailed out". We turned right. The pilot was swinging in his parachute. We then turned left in line with the bomber stream, heading north. Ahead of us a few miles away was another lone aircraft – a "Zeke". We closed on the pilot from behind, and I held my fire until I saw the colonel fire. My gun camera film was reviewed the next day. It pictured the whole aeroplane that quickly exploded as the rounds struck home. For a moment it appeared that I would fly into the flame, but the ruins dropped as I pulled up over it.'

Weather intervened again, forcing the 27 June fighter strike on Nagoya airfields to abort, so the Mustangs tried once more on 1 July. Bad weather again was a factor, making it impossible for the 15th and 506th FGs to attack their targets. But the 21st FG found the conditions over its target – Hamamatsu Airfield – suitable and bored in, firing rockets and machine guns.

After the attack, the group was returning to the Rally Point when it came across a formation of Japanese twin-engined bombers and pounced. The short fight produced three confirmed victories, including one G4M 'Betty' bomber for Maj Harry Crim. This was the fifth kill for the young commander of the 531st FS, making him the newest 'Sun Setter' ace.

THE FINAL ASSAULT

By this time, it was becoming obvious to the 'Sun Setters' that the frequency and numbers of Japanese fighters attempting to intercept the American raids on Honshu were diminishing. This was due in part to losses suffered by the defenders in three months of combat with VII Fighter Command, plus dwindling supplies of fuel. But another factor was the decision by Japanese military leaders to pull most of their forces out of range of the American raiders to save them for use during the Allies' expected invasion of the home islands.

This would not stop the 'Sun Setters' from looking for trouble over Honshu, however. They completed 16 VLR missions in July, which was more than double June's total. But the escort of B-29s, originally planned as VII Fighter Command's primary mission, assumed a lesser role. With aerial opposition drastically reduced except for on a few missions, the eager pilots began attacking targets of opportunity on a much greater scale. Their primary targets continued to be airfields, but they also went after rail transportation, power line installations and shipping. As a result, the Mustangs' exposure to flak rose dramatically.

Short-range strikes against targets in the Bonin Islands, primarily on Chichi Jima, continued as well. Aided in finding targets by the arrival on Iwo of a detachment from a Marine Corps photo-reconnnaissance squadron, VII Fighter Command carried out 45 combat missions, comprising 338 sorties, to the Bonins during July and August 1945.

Although missions to the Bonins were by nature less dangerous than VLR operations, they nevertheless cost the lives of two more P-51 pilots before the end of the war.

The first of these was particularly frustrating because of the tremendous, but ultimately unsuccessful, effort made to save the pilot. It occurred on 3 July, when eight rocket-equipped P-51s of the 15th FG attacked shipping in Futami Harbour, on Chichi. 1Lt Richard H Schroeppel of the 78th FS was flying wingman in the last element over the target when his Mustang was hit and set afire. Low and slow in the

When 1Lt Richard Schroeppel of the 78th FS was shot up over Chichi Jima and bailed out just off the harbour entrance on 3 July, this lifeboat-equipped B-17 was sent from Iwo Jima to try to help. The Higgins boat was dropped successfully to Schroeppel, but it ran aground on a reef close enough to shore that Japanese gunners were able to kill the downed pilot before help arrived (*Harry Reese*)

burning aeroplane, Schroeppel barely had time to bail out and land in the water at the entrance to the harbour. He climbed into his life raft and attempted to paddle out to sea, but the currents carried him north among some rocks close to shore.

While Schroeppel was struggling against the tide, the other aeroplanes in his flight orbited his position and strafed gun positions along the shore that were firing at the downed pilot. Forty more P-51s were despatched from Iwo to aid in the rescue effort, and shortly afterward a B-17 carrying a lifeboat arrived on the scene and dropped it for Schroeppel. The boat grounded on a reef, and Schroeppel was able to reach it, but he was subsequently killed by machine gun fire from the shore. A PBY flying-boat landed and attempted to recover the body, but it was driven off by heavy mortar and machine gun fire.

Ten days later, 2Lt Albert C Marklin of the 462nd FS went down over Chichi as well, possibly the result of one of the rockets carried by his aeroplane exploding while still attached to the wing.

Encounters with Japanese interceptors had diminished, but the Honshu defenders had not given up entirely. As a result, the 'Sun Setters' scored at least one aerial victory in 13 of the 25 VLR missions flown in July and August. Flt Off Anthony J Gance of the 531st FS considered the mission of 6 July – a strafing attack on Atsugi Airfield – his most memorable. This is his recollection;

'I knew this was going to be an exciting mission because I was going to be wingman for Maj Crim, who was our squadron commander. Crim took more chances than most leaders. I knew he was out to become a double ace.

'We got to Japan in less than three hours and started looking for Atsugi Airfield. Crim spotted the base, and within a short time we were over the

P-51D *PROVIDENCE PERMITTIN'* (44-72855) displays eight mission markers in this photograph, taken at South Field prior to its ninth trip. 2Lts Leonard A Dietz and Allen F Colley of the 462nd FS shared the aeroplane, and Dietz recalled that it was named after a favourite saying of Colley's grandmother (*Bill Ebersole*)

1Lt David M Scotford of the 531st FS models the latest in VLR pilots' attire. Scotford was assigned to the squadron fresh out of fighter training in January 1945, and went on to fly nine VLR missions, three to Chichi Jima and numerous combat air patrols. He returned to civilian life after the war, completing his Ph.D. in geology in 1950 and embarking on a teaching career at Miami University, Oxford, Ohio (*Dave Scotford*)

Maj Harry Crim was the 21st FG's solitary ace, finishing the war with six kills and 4.25 damaged to his credit (*Harry Crim*)

target at about 14,000 ft. Crim signalled to get into line abreast. He got us into position and signalled for the attack. We headed in a dive toward one end of the airfield. At a short distance above the ground, we approached a speed of near 500 mph. There was a lot of machine gun fire at us. The tracers were all around us, but none of us got hit. I guess they didn't lead us enough.

'There were a lot of aeroplanes on the ground. We started to fire our guns, and I had two aeroplanes explode as I shot them – all members of our flight shot up aeroplanes. As we came to the end of the field, Crim started a climbing turn. He made a circle and indicated to us that we were going to make another strafing run – most flight leaders didn't do this because the Japs would be ready for us. We made the run and hit more aeroplanes.

'We made our climb, but the other two aeroplanes in our flight apparently lost us. So it was just Crim and I as we climbed over Tokyo Bay.

At about 15,000 ft Crim yelled, "Bogies at 'five o'clock high!'" They were almost at our level. It happened that there were five of them. We both turned to engage, and in short order Crim shot up two aeroplanes and I got one. Crim then shot down another Jap, but I couldn't get the last aeroplane. I knew I was getting low on gas, so I dove and headed for the ocean, where a B-29 was to lead us back to Iwo.

'As I was heading toward the ocean, I saw another aeroplane in the distance. It was coming right at me. I thought I had no recourse but to engage him head-on. Then a voice over the radio said, "Is that you, Gance?" I said, "Yes, sir", to which Crim replied, "Get on my wing and let's go home". The next day, my crew chief said we had expended almost all of our ammo. Also, our gas tanks were just about empty. God and luck had been with us.'

Crim was credited with one Zero confirmed destroyed in the air for his sixth, and last, victory of the war, plus two Zeros and a Raiden damaged. Gance received credit for one Raiden damaged. Also on 6 July, 1Lt Clarence 'Bud' Bell of the 72nd FS was shot down and taken prisoner.

The 7 July mission was a weather abort, and on the 8th the 15th and 506th FGs tallied six victories at a cost of four pilots lost, including one PoW. The 8 July mission was also notable because the Sub Cover flight of the 458th FS – 1Lts Jack Kelsey, Dean Jensen, Ralph Coltman and Francis Pilecki – stayed aloft for more than nine hours in assisting the attempted rescue of a downed pilot just off the coast of Japan.

A fighter strike to Osaka on 9 July netted 13 confirmed victories for the 21st FG. As the group's three squadrons approached the target, they unwittingly sandwiched two large formations of Japanese fighters between the 531st FS, flying top cover, and the 46th and 72nd FSs below.

1Lts James E Coleman and Ralph R Coltman Jr of the 458th FS shared P-51D *MY DARLIN BETTY ANN*, which was named *The Ole Lady* on the port side. As a member of his squadron's Sub Cover Flight on 8 July, Coltman was one of four pilots that stayed aloft for more than nine hours in assisting the attempted rescue of a downed pilot just off the coast of Japan (*Tim Bivens*)

P-51Ds of the 531st FS sit at Central Field with a B-29 behind them. '333' (44-63933) flew throughout the VLR campaign, only to be damaged in a ground loop on 24 September 1945. '302' *JOY'S BOY* (44-63910) had a shorter life, aborting two missions in May, before being destroyed the following month (*Dave Scotford*)

Maj Robert L McDonald, 46th FS CO, climbs into the cockpit of *Pat-Riot* (44-63737) in midsummer 1945. A veteran of combat during the campaign in the Aleutian Islands, McDonald shot down a Japanese floatplane fighter over Kiska in October 1942 while flying P-38s with the 54th FS (*Bob Louwers*)

The 531st dove on the enemy aeroplanes, which split-essed into a thin layer of clouds and came out among the two strike squadrons underneath. A wild melee ensued, as 2Lt G R 'Jerry' Nolin of the 46th FS recalled;

'We had proceeded inland about 50 miles in a generally northern direction in squadron formation when two bogies appeared on our right, coming toward us at about our altitude. I spotted them and called them out. The bogies swung around behind us about three miles, without acting aggressive. My flight whirled around in an extremely tight 180-degree turn and headed toward the bogies. I fired at one of them, starting at too long a range. When he noticed I was firing at him, he made a quick break to the left.

'The quick turnaround at the start had reduced my airspeed too much, and I was going in the wrong direction. I solved both problems at once by doing a split-S. This got me going good again, and in the same direction as the rest of the squadron, which was now somewhat above me.

'The Mustangs were chasing one of the bogies around, and he made a quick dive to escape. He happened to pull out of his dive right in front of me. I just put my gunsight pipper on him and fired. The full force of my

2Lt Gervais R 'Jerry' Nolin of the 46th FS got his best crack at the enemy on 9 July, scoring one confirmed victory, one probable and two damaged near Nagoya. In all, he completed ten VLR missions to Japan, plus three strikes at Chichi Jima and one at Haha Jima, before the end of the war (*Jerry Nolin*)

guns hit the "Tojo". His engine stopped almost instantly. I cut the throttle to avoid overrunning him and drew up alongside the fighter. The pilot was climbing out of the cockpit and bailed out. The fighter continued down, hit the ground and disintegrated in a large ball of flame.'

The 531st FS gained a second ace on 9 July as Capt Willis E Mathews, squadron operations officer, was credited with two victories. Mathews had flown a previous combat tour in P-38s with the 94th FS/1st FG in the MTO, scoring 3.5 victories against the Luftwaffe. He joined the 531st in May 1945 as a replacement pilot, and became ops officer the following month when Capt Charles Betz rotated to the US. Mathews eventually completed 13 VLR missions, left the service after the war and was recalled to fly F-51s during the Korean conflict.

A mix of 46th FS P-51D-20s and D-25s sits on the flightline with three B-24s in the background. *Okey Dokey* and the third Mustang (44-73377) are D-25s, while '238' (44-63432) between them is a D-20. A newer aircraft, '211' displays just three mission markers forward of the cockpit (*Jerry Nolin*)

Lt Col John W Mitchell (third from left in the top row) of VII Fighter Command stands with the 47th FS pilots he led on the 4 July fighter strike against enemy airfields in the Tokyo area. Mitchell gained notoriety in 1943 when he led the P-38 mission from Guadalcanal that shot down the G4M 'Betty' bomber carrying Adm Yamamoto, architect of the Pearl Harbor attack. The arrow at far left points to Flt Off John W Googe (*John Googe*)

VLR missions continued as the weather allowed during July. The 'Sun Setters' struck Tokyo airfields on 10 July, gaining one aerial victory and 15 ground kills for the loss of three P-51s, but no pilots. The 14 July mission was scrubbed by weather, and the following day the 531st FS added four more victories to its scoreboard on a strike in the Nagoya area. An additional nine ground victories were credited, but the 47th FS lost two pilots killed, and one pilot of the 78th FS was shot down and captured.

On 16 July, the 21st and 506th FGs sent 96 Mustangs to attack airfields at Nagoya. One P-51 went down on the outbound flight when a fuel leak set fire to the aeroplane – its pilot bailed out and was rescued. The 21st FG, led by Lt Col Mitchell of VII Fighter Command, was first into the target area and encountered an estimated 60 enemy aircraft before the Mustangs were able to strafe the airfields as originally planned. The 506th FG Mustangs joined the air battle a few minutes later, led by Maj Malcolm 'Muddy' Watters, formerly 457th FS CO, and now serving as group operations officer.

According to VII Fighter Command publication *Fighter Notes*, the Japanese defenders proved more 'aggressive and able' during this aerial combat than on any previous mission. 'However, they did not use mutual support, and our aeroplanes always had the advantage except when they became separated and several Japs could attack a stray Mustang'.

The group reported four Mustangs damaged in the fight, and Capt John W Benbow, 457th FS operations officers, was lost. Members of Capt Benbow's flight did not see him get hit in the dogfight, and thought his P-51 may have been damaged by debris flying off a Japanese aeroplane shot down by the 'Green Flight' leader, Capt William B Lawrence. Subsequent research suggests, however, that Benbow was almost certainly shot down by a Ki-100 flown by one-legged Japanese ace Maj Yohei Hinoki, who was an instructor at the JAAF's Akeno Flying School. Hinoki would survive the war with at least 12 kills to his credit.

For the loss of Capt Benbow, the 'Sun Setters' claimed 25 confirmed victories, two probable victories and 18 aircraft damaged on 16 July. One of the 506th FG pilots claiming his first kills of the war that day was Capt Abner M Aust Jr, a flight commander in the 457th FS. This was his report of the action;

'I was leading "Blue Flight" in the second section of our squadron in the Nagoya area when six bogies were called out at "nine o'clock low". I called my section to drop their tanks, and we peeled off low on a flight of six "Franks". I made almost a head-on pass at their "Number One" man, and gave him a two- or three-second squirt around the cockpit before he broke away to his right. As I turned with him, and left, I was almost on top of another Jap fighter. I split-essed with him and got hits with a three-second burst around the engine and cockpit area. After I passed him, my flight saw him bail out.

457th FS operations officer Capt John W L Benbow went down near Suzuka in P-51D '508' on 16 July – this was his sixth Empire mission. Although none of the other members of his flight saw what happened to him, Benbow was almost certainly shot down by JAAF ace Maj Yohei Hinoki, who claimed one Mustang destroyed that day while flying a Ki-100. No trace of Benbow was ever found (*Ray Miller*)

457th FS 'D Flight' pilots pose with
1Lt Larry Grennan's P-51D *GANG
BANG*. They are, from left top
row, Joe Winn (PoW), Chuck
Veitenheimer, Grennan and Jim
Hinkle, middle row, Ray Miller, Bill
Lawrence (flight commander), Martin
Ganschow and Chet Jatczak, and
bottom row, Alan Kinvig, Omar
Skiver, George Hetland and Joe
Morrison (Ralph Gardner)

Capt Abner M Aust Jr was both a
flight commander in the 457th FS
and the only ace in the 506th FG.
On 16 July he was credited with
three Ki-84 Hayates destroyed over
Nagoya, and in the Sun Setters
last aerial combat of the war, on
10 August, he shot down two A6M
Zeros to raise his victory total to five.
Aust made the Air Force his career
post-war, flying some 300 missions
in Vietnam while commanding an
F-4 Phantom II wing - this
photograph of Aust was taken
during the latter posting

'As I pulled up, another "Frank" was almost in front of me, and when I
closed in on him he split-essed and I followed him. I was getting hits all the
way through, and I finished up with a burst into the cockpit. I believe that
I killed the pilot, because he went straight into the clouds. As I pulled up
another was coming at me almost head-on. I fired a burst into his engine,
and he split-essed and I followed. I closed in on him and got hits in his
right wing root and cockpit. He started smoking and burning in the right
wing and fuselage as he went straight into the clouds.

'We pulled off this one and I was almost behind another. As I closed in,
he split-essed and I followed him as he went into a dive. I got hits in the
root of the left wing, and before he
went into the clouds I saw smoke
coming out of the wing. I fired all my
remaining ammunition at him and
followed him down into the clouds
to about 2000 ft and then pulled up
because we were doing about 350-
375 mph and the elevation of the
ground was about 1000 ft. He was
going almost straight down, and
made no move to shake us. I didn't
believe he could have pulled out.'

In this, the 'Sun Setters'' last big
air battle of the war, Aust was top
scorer with three Ki-84s confirmed

destroyed and three more damaged. Three days later, on 19 July, VII Fighter Command tallied nine more kills, but their one pilot lost was Lt Col Jack Thomas, 15th FG commander. Ever aggressive, Thomas was diving straight down in his attempt to strafe a bomber on Kagamigahara Airfield when his Mustang entered compressibility and shed its wings, carrying the veteran 'Pineapple' pilot to his death. A few days later, Lt Col John Mitchell was appointed the new CO of the 15th FG.

Only one more Japanese aircraft was shot down during the rest of the month, although missions were flown on 20, 22, 24, 28 and 30 July. During the course of these missions, seven more 'Sun Setter' pilots were killed and one was taken prisoner.

Lt Col John Mitchell, who assumed command of the 15th FG when Lt Col Jack Thomas was killed on 19 July 1945, often flew this 78th FS P-51D *Annie* (44-73382). The victory flags are apparently for the aeroplane, as Mitchell claimed three victories while flying with VII Fighter Command which raised his overall total for the war to 11 enemy aircraft confirmed destroyed (*Tom Ivie*)

Acting 47th FS CO Capt Walter H 'Sam' Powell (left) was killed in action on 30 July when he was hit by ground fire while attacking airfields in the Kobe-Osaka area. Here, Powell poses with the crew of *ADAM LAZONGA*, namely crew chief SSgt Emil O Klein (centre) and assistant crew chief Cpl Walter F Martin (*Emil Klein*)

The 414th FG, equipped with long-range Republic P-47N Thunderbolts, arrived on Iwo Jima in July 1945 and completed three VLR missions before the end of the war. This machine, named *Blunderbus* (44-88706), carries the yellow and black checkertail markings of the 437th FS (*Ed Linfante*)

In mid-July, a new fighter type began to appear in the skies around Iwo Jima with the arrival of the P-47N-equipped 414th FG. Sharing North Field with the 506th FG, the 414th initially flew Combat Air Patrol missions in the Iwo vicinity and graduated to Chichi Jima strikes before mounting its first VLR mission on 1 August.

The mission was supposed to be the first four-group strike by VII Fighter Command, but bad weather at Iwo prevented the 15th and 506th FGs from taking off. Following the 21st FG, 21 Thunderbolts of the 414th FG strafed installations on Okazaki and Nagoya East airfields, losing one P-47 and pilot in the process. The 414th FG completed two more VLR missions before the end of the war, and one of its pilots shot down a Ki-46 reconnaissance aircraft while on CAP near Iwo on 4 August.

ON TO VICTORY

News of the nuclear explosion that levelled Hiroshima on 6 August 1945 caught everyone by surprise on Iwo Jima. Sure, there were rumours that America was developing a super bomb like that, but no one really knew anything about it. As far as the 'Sun Setter' pilots had been concerned prior to then, their overriding wish was to complete the 15 VLR missions that would earn them a ticket home. And if they were smart, they were hoping to finish their tours before the actual invasion of Japan started. Now there was reason to expect the Japanese to throw in the towel at any moment.

This aerial portrait of P-51D 44-72856 shows the green tail marking of the 457th FS to good advantage. The fighter, shared by 1Lts William G Hetland and Raymond O Miller, shows the twin 'Uncle Dog' antennae on its spine, radio antennae under the fuselage and bomb-aiming stripes on the wing – features seen of all VII Fighter Command Mustangs operating from Iwo Jima in 1945 (*Ray Miller*)

But the enemy did not collapse immediately, so the 'Sun Setters' continued flying missions to Japan. After hitting airfields in the Tokyo area on 2, 3, 5 and 6 August, and losing eight pilots in the process, VII Fighter Command put up an escort mission to Tokogawa on 7 August and struck airfields at Osaka 24 hours later, losing three more pilots and six P-51s to ground fire. In these six missions, just one enemy aircraft had been shot down.

The last encounter with Japanese fighters came on 10 August, when the 15th and 506th FGs were assigned to escort B-29s to Tokyo. Among the

Capt Jack K Ort of the 46th FS was flying his *"AbORTion"* (44-63898) on 8 August when he was shot down and taken prisoner in the Osaka area. When questioned by the Japanese secret police about the atomic bomb, which had been dropped on Hiroshima two days earlier, Ort could not or would not tell them anything about it, so his furious captors executed him (*Jerry Nolin*)

VII Fighter Command's 'ace of aces', Maj 'Todd' Moore, poses with his P-51D *Stinger VII* in August 1945 (*USAAF*)

115

This side-on shot of Maj 'Todd'
Moore's *Stinger VII* displays the
pilot's full scoreboard after he
claimed his 12th victory on 10
August 1945. This particular P-51D,
formerly named *Tom Cat* when
flown by previous 45th FS CO
Maj Buck Snipes, shows evidence
of repainting in the squadron's
simplified, green late-war markings
(*R W Moore via Tom Ivie*)

seven victories credited to the 'Sun Setters' was one to Maj 'Todd' Moore
of the 45th FS, bringing the ace's victory total to 12, and two to Capt
Abner Aust of the 457th FS, making him the 506th's only ace, and the last
pilot of VII Fighter Command to tally five or more victories.

All four fighter groups headed for Japan on 14 August for what would
be their last combat mission of the war. 1Lt J W 'Bill' Bradbury of the
72nd FS recalled that the mission was postponed for two days while
surrender negotiations were underway before VII Fighter Command was
finally ordered to fly. He recalled the mission;

'We arrived off the coast of Honshu and joined the bomber stream to
escort them over their target. They dropped their bombs, and we went
back out over the ocean to join our three (navigator) B-29s. As we joined
them and started flying back to Iwo Jima, one of the B-29s had picked up
radio transmissions and came on the air saying, "Hey fellows, the war's
over". I remember someone punching their mike button and replying,
"Well the Japs sure as hell don't know it". He was referring to all the flak
that was put up over the target against the bombers. We took about three-
and-a-half hours to fly back to Iwo Jima and landed. Sure enough, the war
was over.'

As best can be determined 60 years after the fact, at the cessation of
hostilities VII Fighter Command had run up a score of 452 Japanese
aircraft destroyed in the air and on the ground. Countless other ground
targets had also been attacked during strafing missions. VII Fighter
Command had paid a high price for this success, however, as 130
Mustangs were lost and 121 men killed or captured, including the victims
of the 26 March banzai raid. But not a single 'Sun Setter' would say the
sacrifice was not worth the final reward of victory in the Pacific.

For the next two weeks flying was restricted to the local area around Iwo
Jima, as everyone awaited word of the actual signing of the peace
agreement. Then on 31 August the 'Sun Setters' were assigned a final VLR
mission to Japan – a 'Display of Power' flight over Japan, led by Col
Harper of the 506th FG. Few were eager to risk another long haul over the
Pacific, and sure enough one pilot, 1Lt William S Hetland of the 457th
FS, experienced engine trouble over the target area. Fortunately, Hetland
made a safe landing at Atsugi Airfield and returned to Iwo aboard a C-46.

The 72nd FS 'Scalpers' scoreboard displayed the full measure of the squadron's toll on the Japanese during the war when this photograph was taken on 15 August. It shows 33 aerial victories and 12 damaged, 25 ground victories and 59 damaged, 14 bombing missions and miscellaneous ground targets destroyed or damaged. *All Pau* is Hawaiian slang for 'finished' or 'all done' (*Bob Sterritt*)

On 2 September, Brig Gen 'Mickey' Moore boarded an LB-30 Liberator transport with orders reassigning him to the Pentagon. Within a week, the most veteran pilots and ground personnel began getting their tickets home as well. VII Fighter Command began shrinking rapidly, and in October pre-separation lectures were instituted for the men.

Late in the year, the headquarters was moved to Guam and redesignated the 20th FW. The 506th FG was deactivated in mid-November and its remaining personnel transferred to the 21st FG, while the 15th FG was

Lt Col Charles E Parsons, who took over as 21st FG CO shortly after the war ended, sits on the wing of 46th FS P-51D '201' (44-72873). The aeroplane's former name *Little Gook II*, has been removed from the cowling panel below the exhausts (*Bob Louwers*)

transferred to Hawaii for deactivation. The 21st FG finally transferred to Saipan in the final weeks of 1945 and then moved to Guam, where it was redesignated the 23rd FG in October 1946.

Between 1952 and 1955, all three VLR groups were again reactivated as USAF fighter wings. The 506th Tactical Fighter Wing was inactivated for good in 1959, however, although the other two – now the 15th Airbase Wing and the 21st Space Wing – continue to serve their nation as this book is written.

And what became of the stinky, depressing and dangerous island of Iwo Jima? American forces continued to serve on Iwo for many years after the armistice. Central Field, formerly home of the 21st FG, was maintained and expanded, while the other two runways were abandoned and allowed to be taken back by nature. American servicemen could still find the bones of Japanese soldiers in Iwo's caves into the early 1950s, and the Marine Corps occasionally used the island to conduct combat exercises. The US Coast Guard established a LORAN (LOng RAnge Navigation) station there as well.

According to recently uncovered information, the US stored nuclear weapons on Iwo Jima (and Chichi Jima) from 1956 until 1966. Then in June 1968 the Bonin and Volcano islands were returned to Japan, becoming part of Ogasawara village in the Tokyo Metropolitan Prefecture. The Japanese Self Defence Force has used Iwo Jima as a patrol and rescue base ever since.

In 1995, the Japanese government allowed a small delegation of Americans to visit the island for a remembrance ceremony marking the 50th anniversary of the historic events that took place there during World War 2.

The flying did not stop for the 'Sun Setters' when the Japanese sued for peace. Here, 1Lts William F Killian and Joseph P Gutierrez Jr take up 78th FS P-51s *JIMMY* (44-63353) and *Sweet Rosalie* (44-72461) for a peaceful photo session over Mt Suribachi. Note that both Mustangs have been repainted in the all-yellow revised squadron markings adopted in midsummer 1945 (*Bill Killion*)

APPENDICES

APPENDIX 1

VLR UNIT COMMANDERS

VII Fighter Command

Brig Gen Ernest M 'Mickey' Moore   -/-/44 to EOW

15th FG

Col James O Beckwith Jr	5/3/43 to 15/5/45
Lt Col DeWitt Spain	15/4/45 to 15/5/45
Lt Col Julian E Thomas	15/5/45 to 19/7/45 (KIA)
Lt Col John W Mitchell	19/7/45 to EOW

45th FS

Maj Gilmer L Snipes	4/4/44 to 16/4/45
Maj Arthur M Bridge	16/4/45 to 3/6/45
Capt Harold D Collins	4/6/45 to 18/7/45
Maj Robert W 'Todd' Moore	19/7/45 to EOW

47th FS

Maj John A Piper	7/11/44 to 26/5/45
Maj Theon E 'Ed' Markham	26/5/45 to 11/6/45
Capt Walter H Powell	11/6/45 to 30/7/45 (KIA)
Capt Ernest W Hostetler	30/7/45 to 4/8/45
Maj Theon E 'Ed' Markham	5/8/45 to EOW

78th FS

Maj James M Vande Hey	14/4/44 to 16/4/45
Maj James B Tapp	16/4/45 to 16/6/45
Capt Joe Fitzsimmons	16/6/45 to 5/8/45
Maj James B Tapp	6/8/45 to EOW

21st FG

Col Kenneth R Powell	21/4/44 to 14/6/45
Lt Col Charles E Taylor	14/6/45 to EOW

46th FS

Maj Fred A Shirley	20/11/44 to 5/45
Maj Benjamin C Warren	5/45 to 6/45
Maj Robert L McDonald	7/45 to EOW

72nd FS

Maj Paul W Imig	-/-/44 to /5/45
Maj James C Van Nada	5/45 to EOW

531st FS

Maj John S 'Sam' Hudson	15/4/44 to 26/3/45 (WIA)
Maj Harry C Crim Jr	31/3/45 to EOW

506th FG

Col Bryan B Harper	10/44 to EOW

457th FS

Maj Malcolm C Watters	10/44 to 1/6/45
Maj Daun G Anthony	2/6/45 to EOW

458th FS

Maj Harrison Shipman	10/44 to EOW

462nd FS

Maj Thomas D DeJarnette	10/44 to EOW

APPENDIX 2

UNIT MARKINGS

All VLR Mustangs were P-51D-20/25s in natural metal with Olive Drab anti-glare panels.

15th FG

The squadrons of the 15th FG began trading their P-47Ds for P-51D-20s in November 1944 while based in Hawaii. The Mustangs were painted with distinct squadron markings while still in Hawaii. In July 1945 all three squadrons simplified their markings, although not all aircraft had been repainted by war's end.

45th FS

The P-51s of the 45th FS were assigned numbers 50 to 99, applied on the fuselage forward of the national insignia in black. They initially had green/black/green propeller spinners, a green 18-inch slanted band with black borders on the upper fin and rudder, and green 18-inch stripes with black borders sweeping out and back on the top of the wings inboard of the pylons and on the tailplanes. Some pilots of the 45th described the markings' colour as 'dark apple green'. Most aircraft carried the squadron badge on both sides of the lower cowling. In the simplified scheme, P-51s had solid green propeller spinners, unbordered green wingtips and horizontal stabilisers and green fin/rudder tops.

47th FS

The P-51s of the 47th FS were assigned numbers 150 to 199, applied on the fuselage forward of the national insignia in black. The markings were yellow/black/yellow propeller spinner, a black band with yellow borders on the rear fuselage behind the national insignia, a black wedge with yellow borders on the upper fin/rudder, and black 18-inch bands with yellow borders around the wings outboard of the pylons and on the tailplanes. Photographic evidence suggests that replacement aircraft carried only a squadron number, with the other markings omitted.

78th FS

The P-51s of the 78th FS were assigned numbers 100 to 149. Early markings consisted of yellow/black propeller spinner, a six-inch black band around the nose behind the spinner, thick bands of yellow above black on the vertical tail, and yellow tips outboard of six-inch black bands on the wings and tailplanes. The 'Bushmasters'' unit badge was painted on the forward fuselage. In the revised paint scheme, the black band was removed from the nose, except where it crossed the anti-glare panel, and the black was overpainted with yellow on the propeller spinner, wings and tail.

21st FG

The squadrons of the 21st FG began trading their P-38s for P-51D-20s in December 1944 while based in Hawaii. The Mustangs were painted in distinct squadron markings while still in Hawaii, and retained them through to the end of the war.

46th FS

The P-51s of the 46th FS were assigned numbers 200 to 249, and the squadron colour was blue. Markings consisted of a blue propeller spinner, a $4^1/_2$-inch black band around the nose behind the spinner, the outboard $14^1/_2$ inches of the wingtips in blue, with a $4^1/_2$-inch black band inboard, the outboard $11^1/_2$ inches of the horizontal stabiliser tips in blue, with a $4^1/_2$-inch black band inboard, and $11^1/_2$-inch blue band around the vertical tail above the serial number, with black $4^1/_2$-inch borders.

72nd FS

The P-51s of the 72nd FS were assigned numbers 250 to 299, and the squadron colour was yellow. Markings consisted of a yellow propeller spinner, a $4^1/_2$-inch black band around the nose behind the spinner, the outboard $14^1/_2$ inches of the

wingtips in yellow, with a $4^1/_2$-inch black band inboard, the outboard $11^1/_2$ inches of the horizontal stabiliser tips in yellow, with a $4^1/_2$-inch black band inboard, and an $11^1/_2$-inch yellow band around the vertical tail above the serial number, with black $4^1/_2$-inch borders.

531st FS

The P-51s of the 531st FS were assigned numbers 300 to 349, and the squadron colour was white. Markings consisted of a white propeller spinner, a $4^1/_2$-inch black band around the nose behind the spinner, the outboard $14^1/_2$ inches of the wingtips in white, with a $4^1/_2$-inch black band inboard, the outboard $11^1/_2$ inches of the horizontal stabiliser tips in white, with a $4^1/_2$-inch black band inboard, and an $11^1/_2$-inch white band around the vertical tail above the serial number, with black $4^1/_2$-inch borders.

506th FG

New P-51D-20/25s arrived in the Marianas with the 506th FG flight detachment in March 1945, and these were painted in squadron markings on Tinian prior to moving up to Iwo Jima in May. Unit markings were applied to the tails.

457th FS

The P-51s of the 457th FS were assigned numbers 500 to 549, and the squadron colour was green. The original markings consisted of 4-inch-wide angled green stripes on the rear fuselage, vertical fin and stabilisers (but not on the rudder or elevators). These were changed to solid green for better visibility shortly after the squadron began combat operations. Some aircraft carried the squadron badge on the rear of the engine cowling on the port side.

458th FS

The P-51s of the 458th FS were assigned numbers 550 to 599, and the squadron colour was blue (probably Dark Sea Blue obtained from the Navy). The original markings consisted of 4-inch-wide angled dark blue stripes on the rear fuselage, vertical fin and stabilisers (but not on the rudder or elevators). Replacement aircraft were painted in solid dark blue, but original aircraft retained their striped tails.

462nd FS

The P-51s of the 462nd FS were assigned numbers 600 to 649, and the squadron colour was yellow. The original markings consisted of 4-inch-wide angled yellow stripes on the rear fuselage, vertical fin and stabilisers (but not on the rudder or elevators). These were changed to solid yellow for better visibility shortly after the squadron began combat operations. Most aircraft carried the squadron badge on the fuselage below the cockpit on the port side.

APPENDIX 3

VLR AERIAL CLAIMS

VII Fighter Command

Lt Col Robert J. Rodgers	0-0-0.5
Maj Howard D Sutterlin	2.5-0-0

15th FG

Lt Col John W Mitchell	3-0-0 (plus 8 kills with 339th FS in 1942-43 and 4 kills with 39th FIS/51st FIW in 1953)
Lt Col Julian E 'Jack' Thomas	1-0-1
Maj Wayne L Wells	3-0-1

45th FS

Capt Arthur H Bridge	0-0.5-0.5
1Lt Wesley E. Brown	2-0-0
2Lt Arthur A Burry	0-0-0.5
Capt Bruce S Campbell Jr	2-0-0
Capt Harold D Collins	1-0-1
1Lt Frederick C Condon	1-0-0.5
1Lt Ceil A Dennis	0-0-0.5
1Lt George H Dunlap	1-0-0.5
1Lt Lloyd C Edwards	0.5-0-0
Capt Francis L Ennis	0.5-0-0.5
1Lt William J Farrell	1-0-0
2Lt Walter Harrigan	0-0.5-0
1Lt Fred H 'Herb' Henderson Jr	1-0.5-0.333
1Lt William H Hodgins	1-0-0
Capt George H Hunter Jr	1.5-1-0
1Lt John E Kester	1-0-0
Capt William L Kester	0-0-0.33 (plus 1.5 kills with 44th FS in 1943)
Capt Morton M Knox	1-0-0 (plus 1 kill on 26/1/44)
Capt Albert E Maltby	1-0-0 (plus 1 probable on 26/1/44)
Capt Robert W 'Todd' Moore	11-1-1 (also with 78th FS, plus 1 kill in 1/44)
2Lt William W. Redus	0-0.5-0
2Lt C Douglas Reese	2-0-0
2Lt Vincent V Reinert	0-0.5-0
1Lt Gerhard C Rettburg	0-1-0
1Lt Joseph G Richins	1-0-0
1Lt Alvan E. Roberts	0.5-0-0
Flt Off Billy J Singleton	0.5-0-0
1Lt Jay W Slater	1.5-2-0
Maj Gilmer L Snipes	1-1-0 (plus 1 kill in 10/43)
1Lt William H Sparks	0.5-0-0

1Lt Donald E Statsman	3-0.5-0.333
2Lt Robert M Thornton	0-0-1
1Lt Joe D Walker	1-1-2
2Lt Leroy E Yakish	0.5-0-0

47th FS

Maj Truman F Anderson	1-0-0
1Lt Frank L Ayres	1-1-0
1Lt Harold L Baccus	1-0-2
1Lt Bernard P Bjorseth	0.5-0-0.5
1Lt Eurich L Bright	3.5-0-0
2Lt Robert C Burnett	1-0-0
1Lt Charles J Cameron	2-1-0
1Lt Richard J Condrick	1-0-1
Capt Robert R Down	1.5-0-0
2Lt Andrew C Elliott	0-0-1
Flt Off John W Googe	0-0-1
1Lt Fred T Grover	3.5-0-0
1Lt Richard H Hintermeier	2.5-0-0 (plus 1 kill with 45th FS in 1/44)
Flt Off Fronnie A Jones Jr	1-0-0
1Lt Roy E June	0.5-0-0.5
Maj Emmett L Kearney Jr	2.5-0-0
Capt Theon E Markham	2.5-0-0
1Lt Joseph A McCormick	0-0-1.5
1Lt George N Metcalf	1-0-0
1Lt Jules C Mitchell	1-0-0
1Lt Stanley A Moore	0-0-1
2Lt Albert G Olivier Jr	0-0-1.5
1Lt Oliver E O'Mara Jr	0.5-0-2
1Lt George C Petrouleas	0.5-0-0
Maj John A Piper	0.5-0-0
Flt Off Harold E Powell	0-0-0.5
Capt Walter H Powell	1-1-0
1Lt Warren G Reed Jr	1-1-0
1Lt Henry C Ryniker	0.5-0-0
1Lt Robert S Scamara	4-1-6
1Lt ? Stelling	0-0-0.5
1Lt Harry M. Tyler	1-0-0
2Lt Robert A. Worton	4-0-0

78th FS

1Lt Frederick A Bauman	1-0-0
1Lt Doyle T Brooks	2-0-1
1Lt Robert Carey	1-0-1
1Lt Robert Carr	0.5-0-0
1Lt Robert C Coryell	2-0-0

1Lt Richard D Duerr	1-0-2	
Capt Joe Fitzsimmons	1.5-0-0	
2Lt James F Hawkins	0-0.5-0	
1Lt Walter W Kreimann	1-0-0	
1Lt Philip J Maher	1-1-0	
1Lt Paul A Martin	0-1-0	
2Lt Daniel Mathis	0.5-0-0	
2Lt Thomas L McCullough	1.5-0-0	
Capt Nelson P Merrill Jr	1-0.5-1	
Capt Victor K Mollan	1.5-0-0	
1Lt Richard Schroeppel	0.5-0-1	
1Lt Malcolm M Sedam	0.5-0-1	
1Lt Robert F Sherbundy	0-1-0	
Maj James B Tapp	8-0-2	
Maj James M Vande Hey	1-0-0 (plus 2 kills with 45th FS in 1/44)	
1Lt Robert L Williams	0.5-0-0	
1Lt Jerome Yellin	0.5-1-1	

21st FG

Lt Col Elmer E Booth	0.5-0-0
Maj Charles J Chapin	1-0-0
Capt Howard J Kendall	1-0-0

46th FS

1Lt John W Brock	3-0-1
1Lt Joseph D Coons	1.5-0-1
1Lt John H Dunn	0-0-1
2Lt Frank Garcia	1-0-0
Capt J V Garnett	0-1-0
1Lt Louis C Gelbrich	1-0-0
1Lt Judd Hoff	0-0-1
2Lt Billy J Knauff	0-0-1
1Lt Russell L Mayhew	0-1-0
1Lt Robert V Merklein	1-0-0
1Lt Eugene A Naber	1-0-0
2Lt Gervais R Nolin	1-1-3
Capt Jack K Ort	1-0-0
1Lt Walter R Parsley	1.5-0-0
Capt Charles O Rainwater	3-0-0
2Lt Morgan R Redwine	0-0-1
2Lt Burdette F Robinson	0-0-1
Maj Fred A Shirley	4-0-0
1Lt Richard L Vroman	1-0-0
1Lt Paul H Wine	1-1-0

72nd FS

2Lt Albert J Allard	1.5-0-1
2Lt James Bradbury	0.5-0-0
2Lt Horace R Brandenberger	1.5-0-0
Capt Adolf J Bregar	2-0-0

2Lt Howard C Brown	1-0-0	
1Lt Ritchfield J S Cameron	0-0-1	
Capt James C Carlyle	1-1-1.5 (plus 2 kills in 12/43)	
1Lt Thomas W Denman	1.5-1-0	
2Lt Chester F Fitzgerald	0-0-1	
1Lt Jacob W Gotwals Jr	1-0-0	
2Lt Claude A Lane	0-0-1	
Capt Ernest S McDonald	1-0-0	
1Lt William E Merritt	3-0-0	
1Lt Harry W Norton	1-0-0	
2Lt Harrison V Parker	0.5-0-0	
2Lt Louis A Pendergrass	1-0-2	
1Lt William A Robinson	1-0-1	
Capt Howard L Russell	1.5-0-0	
2Lt John E Skripek	1.5-0-0	
2Lt Robert S Starr	1-0-0	
2Lt Alfred V Stuart	3-0-0	
Capt James C Van Nada	1-0-0 (plus 1 kill in 12/43)	
Capt Harry E Walmer	2-0-0	
1Lt Horace Wallace	0-0-1	

531st FS

2Lt Lloyd L. Bosley	1-0-0
2Lt Jack Counts	1-0-0
Capt Edwind R Crane	0-0-1.25
Maj Harry C Crim Jr	6-0-4.25
2Lt Earl D Crutchfield	0-0.5-0
1Lt Albert B Davis	1-0-0
1Lt Edward H Dibble	1-0-0
Capt Theodore H Fox	1-0-0.25
Flt Off Anthony J Gance	0-0-1
Capt Vincent A Gaudiani	0-0-1
Capt Frederick J Gibson	1-0-0
2Lt Henry J Koke	1-1-0
2Lt William B Litcher	0-0-1.5
Capt Robert I Mallin	1-0-0
Capt Floyd L Manning	1-0-0 (plus 0.25 kill with 72nd FS in 12/43)
1Lt Wade W Marsh	1-0-0
Capt Willis E Mathews	2-2-2.5 (plus 3.5 kills with 94th FS in 1943)
1Lt Conrad E Mattson	1-0-0
1Lt Floyd E Rice	0-0.5-0
Flt Off Armand G Rowley	1-0-0
1Lt Frank L Seymour	0-0-1
2Lt Roy K Shoemaker	0-0-1
2Lt Irvin P Skansen	0-0-1
1Lt Fred H Sickler Jr	0-0-2
2Lt John D Thompson	2-1-2

2Lt John M Tomlinson — 0-0-1
2Lt John D Wilson — 2-0-0.25

506th FG

Lt Col Harley Brown — 0-0-1
Maj Malcolm C Watters — 2-1-1 (plus 1 kill with 457th FS)

457th FS

1Lt Francis C Albrecht — 1-0-0
Maj Daun G Anthony — 0-0-1
Capt Abner M Aust Jr — 5-0-3
1Lt Thomas W Carroll — 1-0-2
2Lt Walter J Cawley — 0-0-1
Capt Francis B Clark — 0-0-2
2Lt George C Donnelly — 0-0-1
2Lt Ralph S Gardner — 1-0-0.5
2Lt William G Hetlund — 0-0-0.5
2Lt Jackie M Horner — 0-0-1
1Lt William B Lawrence Jr — 1-0-0.5
1Lt Wesley A Murphey Jr — 1-0-1
1Lt Chauncey A Newcomb — 2-0-0
2Lt Clement S Ross — 0-0-1
1Lt Omar K Skiver — 0-0-1.5
2Lt Thomas O Wessell — 0-0-1

458th FS

Capt J B Baker Jr — 1-1-0
Capt Richard W Barnes — 2-0-0
Capt Francis C Carmody — 1-0-0

1Lt Harold G Davidson — 2-0-0
2Lt Raymond Feld — 1-0-0
1Lt Jack A Kelsey — 1-0-0
2Lt Roy E Kempert — 1-0-0
2Lt G B Lambert — 0-1-0
1Lt Quarterman Lee Jr — 1-0-0
1Lt Vance A Middaugh — 1-0-0
1Lt Edward H Mikes Jr — 1-0-0
Capt Peter Nowick — 2-0-0
1Lt Max E Ruble — 1-0-0
2Lt Henry J Seegers Jr — 1-0-0
1Lt Vaughan E Sowers — 1-0-0
1Lt Myndret S Starin — 1-0-0
1Lt Evan S Stuart — 2-1-1
2Lt Frank H Wheeler — 2-0-1

462nd FS

1Lt Edward F Balhorn — 0-0-1
1Lt Darrell S Bash — 1-0-0
1Lt Frank C Buzze — 1-0-0
2Lt Allen F Colley — 0-0-1.5
Maj Thomas D DeJarnette — 1-0-0
1Lt Gordon C Dingee — 1-0-0
1Lt William J Jutras Jr — 1-0-0
Capt Francis L Lee — 1-0-0
Capt Norman T Miller — 1-0-1
2Lt James E Rosebrough — 1-0-0
Capt Frederick A Sullivan — 1-0-1

Unspecified flight — 1-0-0

123

COLOUR PLATES

1
P-51D-20 44-64015 of Col James O Beckwith, 15th FG CO, Airfield No 1, Iwo Jima, April 1945
This P-51D-20 was the last of a long line of *Squirts* flown by Jim Beckwith during World War 2. He progressed from a P-40E, which borrowed its name from the nickname for Beckwith's baby daughter in early 1942, through P-47s and P-51s he flew in Hawaii and then more Mustangs on Iwo Jima. He was assigned 44-64015 after his previous *Squirt* Mustang was destroyed in the crash-landing of a B-29 on Iwo Jima in the spring of 1945. This aircraft passed to Beckwith's successor as 15th FG commander, Lt Col Julian 'Jack' Thomas, in May 1945. Thomas was killed in the fighter, which had possibly be renamed *Jickie* for his wife, over Japan on 19 July 1945.

2
P-51D-20 44-63483 of Maj Gilmer L 'Buck' Snipes, 45th FS/15th FG, Airfield No 1, Iwo Jima, March 1945
'Buck' Snipes was one of the many 45th FS pilots who had flown P-40Ns with the unit in the Central Pacific during 1943-44. He scored the squadron's first confirmed victory of the war when he downed a H8K 'Emily' flying-boat off Baker Island on 23 October 1943. Promoted to command of the 45th FS in April 1944, Snipes was credited with shooting down a Ki-44 'Tojo' on the first VLR mission to Tokyo on 7 April 1945. When Snipes rotated to the US later that month, his *TOM CAT* was passed to Maj 'Todd' Moore, who renamed it.

3
P-51D-20 (serial unknown) of 2Lt C Douglas Reese, 45th FS/15th FG, Airfield No 1, Iwo Jima, July 1945
Doug Reese joined the 45th FS straight out of training in September 1944 at Bellows Field, Hawaii. His first assigned P-51D was '63', which he named for the Biblical figure Shadrach, but that aeroplane was reassigned when Reese went on rest leave from Iwo Jima in April 1945. Upon his return in May, Reese was assigned Mustang '77', and he recalled that the name of the fighter – *SAN ANTONIO ROSE* – had been chosen by its former pilot before he was lost on a mission while flying a different aircraft. Although Reese, who hailed from New Jersey, did not think much of the name, he was very happy to have inherited a top crew chief in Sgt Harold Harless when assigned the Mustang. Reese scored victories on 26 June and 8 July 1945. Unfortunately, the last three digits of his P-51D-20's serial number remain unknown.

4
P-51D-20 44-63483 of Maj R W 'Todd' Moore, 45th FS/15th FG, Airfield No 1, Iwo Jima, August 1945
Destined to become the leading VLR ace, 'Todd' Moore transferred between the 78th FS and the 45th FS several times during the war, before assuming command of the latter unit on 19 July 1945. He scored 11 VLR victories, plus an earlier kill in the Central Pacific campaign while flying a P-40N. *Stinger VII*, which had been the mount of previous 45th FS commander 'Buck' Snipes (see profile 2), shows the effect of the squadron's change to simplified markings during the latter stages of the VLR campaign.

5
P-51D-20 44-63822 of Capt Walter H 'Sam' Powell, 47th FS/15th FG, Airfield No 1, Iwo Jima, April 1945
'Li'l Butch' is one of the most recognised of all VLR P-51s due to the numerous publications of a photograph showing it with the starboard landing gear strut damaged after Capt 'Sam' Powell ground-looped the fighter on take-off for the 12 April 1945 VLR mission. On 30 July, Powell was flying '188' *ADAM LAZONGA* when he was hit by ground fire over Japan. He nursed the Mustang out to sea, but it nose-dived into the water as he was attempting bail out, carrying the acting CO of the 47th FS to his death.

6
P-51D-20 44-63972 of 1Lt W Hayden Sparks, 47th FS/15th FG, Airfield No 1, Iwo Jima, May 1945
Black Rufe is a good example of the many 47th FS machines named after characters in the Al Capp comic strip 'Li'l Abner'. The aeroplane was one of five from the 47th FS that were lost in a tremendous storm on 1 June 1945 while en route to Japan. Fortunately for 1Lt Sparks, he was not assigned to fly on this ill-fated mission.

7
P-51D-20 44-63619 of 1Lt Harry M Tyler, 47th FS/15th FG, Airfield No 1, Iwo Jima, August 1945
When the 47th FS simplified its unit markings in the summer of 1945, it simply removed all colour from its P-51s, as evidenced by *DANNY DAWGMEAT*. Besides the factory-applied markings, all that remained were the name and squadron badge on the port cowling, plus the name and a cartoon portrait of 'Danny Dawgmeat', painted by squadron artist SSgt James N Lindsay, on the opposite side of the aircraft.

8
P-51D-20 44-63973 of Maj James M Vande Hey, 78th FS/15th FG, Airfield No 1, Iwo Jima, April 1945
A survivor of the Pearl Harbor attack, Jim Vande Hey was another of the highly experienced veteran fighter pilots who helped VII Fighter Command get off to such a strong start when it commenced operations from Iwo Jima. He had scored his first two victories on 26 January 1944 while flying a P-40N with the 45th FS during the Central Pacific campaign. On 7 April 1945 Vande Hey knocked down a twin-engined Japanese aeroplane, believed to have been a 'Dinah', while flying *Jeanne VIII* on the first VLR mission to Tokyo. Vande Hey retired from the USAF in 1971, having attained the rank of brigadier general.

9
P-51D-20 44-63353 of 1Lt Doyle T Brooks Jr, 78th FS/15th FG, Airfield No 1, Iwo Jima, June 1945
1Lt Brooks joined the 78th FS in February 1944, and spent nearly a year flying P-40s, P-47s and P-51s over Hawaii prior to deploying to Iwo Jima with the squadron. The flying experience served him well, for on 10 June 1945 he shot down two Japanese fighters and damaged a third while on an escort mission to Tokyo. After the war Brooks became an aeronautical engineer, retiring as chief of structures at Chance Vought Corporation.

10

P-51D-25 44-72641 of 2Lt Joseph P Gutierrez, 78th FS/ 15th FG, Airfield No 1, Iwo Jima, September 1945

A native New Yorker, Gutierrez was assigned to the 78th FS as a replacement pilot on 17 May 1945. *Sweet Rosalee* displays the modified markings adopted by the 78th FS in midsummer 1945. Note how the black stripes on the spinner, wings and tail have been painted over in yellow, and the black nose band has been removed, except for the portion that crossed over the anti-glare panel.

11

P-51D-20 44-63755 of Maj Fred A Shirley, 46th FS/21st FG, Airfield No 2, Iwo Jima, April 1945

Leading scorer of the 46th FS with four confirmed victories, Shirley had gained combat experience with the 45th FS during the Central Pacific campaign, before assuming command of the 46th FS in November 1944. He was credited with destroying a Ki-45 'Nick' and a J2M 'Jack' on the 12 April 1945 Tokyo mission, as well as two more 'Jacks' ten days later over Nagoya, before joining the first contingent of veteran pilots to return to the US from Iwo Jima. P-51D 44-63755 was transferred to the 72nd FS in June, but was lost in combat with Flt Off Philip B Ingalls (who was killed) at the controls on 1 August 1945.

12

P-51D-20 44-63719 of 1Lt Victor F Kilkowski, 46th FS/ 21st FG, Airfield No 2, Iwo Jima, May 1945

1Lt Kilkowski joined the 46th FS straight out of the P-51 Replacement Training Unit at Sarasota, Florida, in March 1945. He flew missions through to the end of the war, when he transferred with the 46th to Saipan and later Guam, before returning home in April 1946. Kilkowski joined the Maryland Air National Guard later that year, and served until 1983, when he retired as a brigadier general. Kilkowski named his P-51D *Little MAGGIE* for his wife.

13

P-51D-20 44-63898 of Capt Jack K Ort, 46th FS/21st FG, Airfield No 2, Iwo Jima, August 1945

A capable flight leader with one confirmed victory, Ort was shot down by groundfire in his P-51 *"abORTion"* near Osaka on 8 August 1945. He parachuted safely and was taken prisoner, but Japanese officers subsequently executed him and four other American aircrew because they were unwilling, or unable, to divulge any information about the atomic bomb that had been dropped on Hiroshima a few days earlier.

14

P-51D-20 44-63451 of 1Lt Robert J Louwers, 46th FS/ 21st FG, Airfield No 2, Iwo Jima, June 1945

A replacement pilot, 1Lt Louwers had 140 hours in P-40s and another 82 hours in P-51s when he arrived on Iwo Jima. In addition to flying nine VLR missions to Japan and one mission over Chichi Jima, he served as photography officer for the 46th FS. The pin-up painting (see scrap view on page 46) on the fuselage of Louwers' P-51D, named for his wife, was rare among 46th FS machines.

15

P-51D-20 44-63733 of Maj Paul W Imig, 72nd FS/21st FG, Airfield No 2, Iwo Jima, April 1945

Paul Imig was an old-timer in VII Fighter Command, having been a member of the first contingent of the 333rd FS that went to Canton Island in late 1942 to defend it with their P-39s. He was then posted to Australia, where he offered to take a demotion if the Fifth Air Force would assign him to combat. The offer rejected, Imig returned to Hawaii and was given command of the 72nd FS, which he subsequently led to Iwo Jima. After more than three years overseas, Imig finally completed several combat missions over Japan, before returning to the US. Named for the woman who would become Imig's wife, *Dede Lou* went on to fly 26 missions with just one abort for a radio problem.

16

P-51D-20 44-63756 of 1Lt Robert C Sterritt, 72nd FS/ 21st FG, Airfield No 2, Iwo Jima, August 1945

Originally slated for duty in the ETO, 1Lt Sterritt was among a group of 16 pilots with P-51 experience who were shipped to Iwo Jima at the end of June 1945 to replace combat losses. After three warm-up missions to Chichi Jima in July, Sterritt flew his first and last VLR mission on 1 August 1945, strafing a railway marshalling yard on the outskirts of Nagoya. By war's end, he had logged 60 hours of combat flight time.

17

P-51D-20 44-63975 of 1Lt Clarence H 'Bud' Bell, 72nd FS/ 21st FG, Airfield No 2, Iwo Jima, July 1945

1Lt Bell had a rough time on VLR operations. After surviving the Japanese banzai attack against the 21st FG tent area in the pre-dawn hours of 26 March 1945, he flew several VLR missions before being shot down on 1 July 1945 on a fighter sweep over Tokorozawa airfield. Hit by flak at about 10,000 ft, he continued his strafing pass before his engine failed and he bailed out over Sagami Bay. Bell was captured and spent the rest of the war in a PoW camp. *Fertile Myrtle* completed five missions and aborted three others before going down on the 1 July mission with Bell at the controls.

18

P-51D-25 44-73623 of Maj Harry C Crim Jr, 531st FS/ 21st FG, Airfield No 2, Iwo Jima, July 1945

Having completed a combat tour flying P-38s in the MTO without scoring any victories, Crim joined the 21st FG in Hawaii as operations officer of the 72nd FS in August 1944. He transferred to the 531st FS as CO after his predecessor, Maj 'Sam' Hudson, was wounded in the 26 March banzai raid. Crim quickly made a name for himself as an aggressive combat leader, and he went on the score six confirmed aerial victories. One of three P-51D-25 replacements delivered to the squadron from Guam in late May 1945, *My Achin!* was Crim's second Mustang in the 531st.

19

P-51D-20 44-63781 of Capt Charles G Betz, 531st FS/ 21st FG, Airfield No 2, Iwo Jima, May 1945

Betz flew combat with the 72nd FS in P-39s during the Central Pacific campaign, claiming one 'Zeke' damaged on 23 December 1943. He transferred to the 531st FS as assistant operations officer in spring 1944 when the squadron transitioned from A-24 dive-bombers to fighters, and became operations officer when Capt Lloyd Whitley was killed in the 24 March 1945 banzai raid. Capt Betz flew the early VLR missions with the 531st before receiving orders sending him home on 1 June 1945. His replacement as operations officer was future ace Capt Willis E Mathews.

20

P-51D-20 44-63934 of 1Lt John F Galbraith, 531st FS/ 21st FG, Airfield No 2, Iwo Jima, June 1945

John Galbraith joined the 531st FS when it was flying P-39s in Hawaii, and he went through the subsequent transitions to the P-38 and P-51. He was credited with shooting nine Japanese soldiers during the 26 March 1945 banzai raid, before being wounded by a grenade blast, but he soon rejoined the squadron and began flying VLR missions. Galbraith shot up a Japanese utility aeroplane near Tokyo on 19 April 1945, but most vividly recalls strafing Japanese picket boats that had been closing in on an American submarine. Galbraith said he flew P-51D '313' because everyone else in the 531st FS was too superstitious to go near it.

21

P-51D-20 44-72557 of 1Lts John W Winnen and Philip G Alston, 457th FS/506th FG, Airfield No 3, Iwo Jima, summer 1945

'527' is a prime example of how the Mustangs of the 506th FG were more highly decorated than those of the other two VLR groups. In most cases, two pilots shared a P-51, and each marked one side of the aircraft. Here, 1Lt Winnen named *HEL-ETER* for his wife Helen and son Peter. On the starboard side, 1Lt Alston named the plane *LIL – TODDIE* after his daughter, with artwork of a toddy glass pouring whiskey over a bomb. The origin of *Lou Flo* is unknown. This aeroplane was lost in August while Alston was on rest leave in Hawaii.

22

P-51D-20 44-63291 of 1Lt Wesley A Murphey Jr, 457th FS/ 506th FG, Airfield No 3, Iwo Jima, Summer 1945

1Lt Murphy's '531' carries the striped green tail markings that were applied to the 457th FS P-51s before the change was made to solid green. It also has the incomplete squadron badge seen on many 457th Mustangs. 1Lt Murphey earned the victory flag on 16 July 1945 when he shot down a 'Tojo' and damaged a 'Zeke' over Nagoya.

23

P-51D-25 44-72854 of Capts William B Lawrence Jr and Alan J Kinvig, 457th FS/506th FG, Airfield No 3, Iwo Jima, summer 1945

The name on this P-51 – *KWITCHERBITCHIN* – may have derived from the fact that its pilots were flight commanders who heard more than their fair share of complaining from the pilots they led. The victory flag was Capt Lawrence's, representing the unidentified single-engined aircraft he shot down on the Nagoya mission of 16 July 1945. He also damaged a 'Tojo' on 10 June. Capt Kinvig, veteran of a previous tour in the Aleutian Islands, had no aerial combat claims.

24

P-51D-20 44-72607 of Maj Harrison E Shipman, 458th FS/ 506th FG, Airfield No 3, Iwo Jima, May 1945

This P-51 had a very short operational life. Although assigned to Maj Shipman, '550' was being flown by Lt Col

Harvey Scandrett when it went down in a storm on the disastrous 1 June 1945 mission. Scandrett, deputy commander of the 506th FG, was leading the group and lost his life that day, along with 23 other VII Fighter Command pilots. Shipman commanded the 458th FS throughout its combat history.

25

P-51D-20 44-72561 of 1Lt Edward H Mikes Jr, 458th FS/ 506th FG, Airfield No 3, Iwo Jima, summer 1945

This was the second P-51 assigned to 1Lt Mikes, who had a rather prominent nose and named the fighter after his wife! Having downed a Japanese fighter on 10 June 1945, Mikes was forced to parachute from his disabled P-51 into Sagami Bay on 3 August, where the American submarine USS *Aspro* picked him up in a daring rescue while a fierce air battle raged overhead.

26

P-51D-20 44-72558 of 1Lt Bennett C Commer and 2Lt Henry J Seegers Jr, 458th FS/506th FG, Airfield No 3, Iwo Jima, summer 1945

1Lt Commer was in the original cadre of pilots assigned to the 458th FS in October 1944. He and Seegers were assigned to 'A Flight', alternating missions in '556'. Commer, who hailed from Mississippi, named the aeroplane *The Boll Weevil* after a common pest back home. On the starboard side, Seegers called it *A Neat Package*, complete with pin-up artwork and a victory flag for the Japanese fighter he shot down on 10 June 1945.

27

P-51D-20 44-72547 of Maj Thomas D DeJarnette, 462nd FS/506th FG, and Lt Col Harley Brown, Deputy CO of the 506th FG, Airfield No 3, Iwo Jima, summer 1945

The pilots who shared *TALLAHASSEE LASSIE* were well acquainted, having flown combat together in P-39s with the 80th FS/8th FG in New Guinea during 1942-43. Their combat experience and leadership served the 506th FG well, as DeJarnette shot down a 'Tony' on 10 June 1945 and Brown damaged a 'Frank' on 19 July. DeJarnette went on to command the famed 4th FIG in 1953 at the end of the Korean conflict, and retired from the USAF in 1970, while Brown became a successful attorney in Wisconsin. '600', like most 462nd Mustangs, displays the squadron insignia designed by pilot Bob Torgerson.

28

P-51D-20 44-72588 of 1Lts Edward J Linfante and Darrell S Bash, 462nd FS/506th FG, Airfield No 3, Iwo Jima, summer 1945

The pilots of *SHANGHAI LIL* were members of the original cadre of aircrew assigned to the 462nd FS. 1Lt Linfante initially flew another P-51, and named '616' for his fiancé when he was reassigned to the new aircraft. The victory flag accrues to 1Lt Bash, who was flying the P-51 when he shot down a Ki-61 'Tony' over Yokohama on 10 June 1945.

29

P-51D-20 44-72587 of 2Lts James R Bercaw and William G Ebersole, 462nd FS/506th FG, Airfield No 3, Iwo Jima, summer 1945

Would shooting up an outhouse while a Japanese soldier was using it constitute an honest mistake?! 2Lts Bercaw and Ebersole obviously thought so. Ebersole, who was youngest pilot in the 462nd FS, joined the squadron in Florida shortly before it departed for Iwo Jima. He flew ten VLR missions to the Japanese mainland and two strikes against Chichi Jima. On 23 June 1945, Ebersole destroyed a twin-engined bomber that was parked on an airfield northeast of Tokyo.

30
P-51D-25 44-72855 of 1Lts Allen F Colley and Leonard A Dietz, 462nd FS/506th FG, Airfield No 3, Iwo Jima, summer 1945
'Providence Permittin'' was a favourite saying of 1Lt Colley's grandmother. Jack Crapser, crew chief of '643', said the aeroplane briefly carried the name *Crapser's Crapper* on the starboard side until Colley asked him to remove it! '643's' two pilots joined the 462nd on the same day – 4 January 1945 – in Florida. Colley was credited with two Japanese fighters damaged on 26 June 1945 and a third damaged on 19 July – the same day Dietz shot up a 'Tojo'. Dietz earned a master's degree in physics in 1950, and went on to enjoy a distinguished career as a physicist and research scientist.

BIBLIOGRAPHY

ANDRADE, JOHN M *US Military Aircraft Designations and Serials Since 1909*

BELL, DANA *Air Force Colors, Volume 3*

CHANT, CHRIS *The Pictorial History of Air Warfare*

DAVIS, LARRY *Bent & Battered Wings, Volume 2*

ETHELL, JEFFREY *Mustang, Documentary History*

HESS, WILLIAM N *Fighting Mustang –The Chronicle Of The P-51*

KINZEY, BERT *P-51 Mustang Detail & Scale, Part 2*

LAMBERT, JOHN W *The Long Campaign – The History of the 15th Fighter Group in World War II*

LAMBERT, JOHN W *The Pineapple Air Force – Pearl Harbor to Tokyo*

MORRISON, WILBUR H *Point of No Return*

OLYNYK, FRANK J *USAAF Credits (Pacific Theater) For The Destruction of Enemy Aircraft in Air-To-Air Combat World War II*

ROSCOE, THEODORE *On the Seas and In The Skies*

RUST, KENN C *The Seventh Air Force Story*

RUST, KENN C *The Twentieth Air Force Story*

SAKAI, SABURO *Samurai!*

SAKAIDA, HENRY *Imperial Japanese Navy Aces, 1937-45*

SAKAIDA, HENRY *Japanese Army Air Force Aces, 1937-45*

SNYDER, LOUIS L *The War, A Concise History 1939-1945*

STANAWAY, JOHN *Mustang and Thunderbolt Aces of the Pacific and CBI*

THOMPSON, WARREN *P-61 Black Widow Units of World War 2*

THORPE, DONALD W *Japanese Army Air Force Camouflage and Markings World War II*

THORPE, DONALD W *Japanese Naval Air Force Camouflage and Markings World War II*

WHELAN, JAMES R *Hunters In The Sky*

INDEX

References to illustrations are shown in **bold**. Plates are shown with page and caption locators in brackets.